DATE DUE

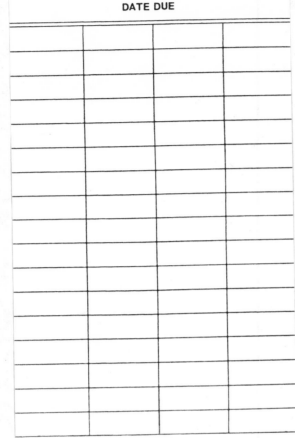

HIGHSMITH 45-220

WITHDRAWN
WRIGHT STATE UNIVERSITY LIBRARY

AMA

erican Management Association

TYING THE CORPORATE KNOT

D1299432

An
American
Management
Association
Research
Report on

The Effects of Mergers and Acquisitions

with the
cooperation of

Control Data Business Management Services

AMA Briefings & Surveys

Don Lee Bohl, Editor

Eric Rolfe Greenberg, Project Director

Anne E. Skagen, Associate Editor

Yvette DeBow, Editorial Associate

Jerry Beilinson, Editorial Associate

HD
2746.5
.T95
1989

Library of Congress Cataloging-in-Publication Data

Tying the corporate knot : an American Management Association research
 report on the effects of mergers and acquisitions / Don Lee Bohl,
 editor ... [et al.].
       p.   cm. -- (AMA briefings & surveys)
     ISBN 0-8144-3520-3 $50.00 ($45.00 to members)
       1. Consolidation and merger of corporations--Planning.   I. Bohl,
 Don Lee. II. American Management Association. III. Series.
 HD2746.5.T95 1989
   658.1'6--dc19   88-37674

© 1989 AMA Membership Publications Division
American Management Association, New York,
New York

All rights reserved. Printed in the United States
of America.

This survey has been distributed to all members
enrolled in the General Management, Finance,
General and Administrative Services, Human
Resources, and Information Services and
Technology divisions of the American
Management Association. Copies may be
purchased at the following single-copy rates:
AMA members: $45; nonmembers: $50.

This publication may not be reproduced, stored
in a retrieval system, or transmitted in whole or
in part, in any form or by any means,
electronic, mechanical, photocopying,
recording, or otherwise, without the prior
written permission of AMA Membership
Publications Division, 135 West 50th Street,
New York, New York 10020.

First Printing

Contents

Foreword

Problems of Change and Implications for Management

by Norbert J. Kubilus

Mergers, acquisitions, consolidations, and divestitures are creating a "service crisis" in the United States as tens of thousands of jobs have been lost because of these organizational changes in the last five years, and an untold number of other individuals have left the surviving entities rather than wait to see if their positions would survive or be cut. An earlier American Management Association research report, *Responsible Reductions in Force*, found that mergers and acquisitions were a factor in 11 percent of workforce reductions, and *Management Review* reported in January 1987 that "middle managers and technical professionals" are among the hardest hit following a corporate reorganization.

Roundtable discussions among information systems executives about the effect of mergers, acquisitions, consolidations, and divestitures on their human resources and information systems have generated comments such as:

- The unwritten contract that said "if you do a good job for us, you've got a job for life" has been broken;
- The uncertainty and personal nervousness that accompany these organizational changes result in lost productivity and turnover while people wait for the other shoe to fall;
- The technical staff remaining in the newly formed organization frequently stops caring, takes longer to perform routine functions, and is less likely to come up with innovative solutions to problems;
- Lots of time is spent on financial and marketing plans before a deal is made, but human resources and information systems are not given serious attention until much later;

■ The level of effort to merge or divest information systems is often ignored until *after* the decision is made to move forward with the organizational change.

The data collected in this new American Management Association study, conducted with the cooperation of Control Data Business Management Services, confirm much of the anecdotal evidence that has been presented in recent years and shed some light on how the planning for mergers, acquisitions, consolidations, and divestitures might be changed in order to avoid many of the problems reported. Many of these problems would be avoidable if only more attention were paid up front to human resource issues and conflicting system architectures.

CONSOLIDATING FOUR ACQUISITIONS

In late 1981, I was vice president for systems development and operations for a company that was going to merge with one of its larger competitors. There were financial and product reasons for the acquisition, but we were told that the new parent was really interested in our systems and technology expertise, which would be critical to the growth of the combined companies. Over the four months that passed from the merger announcement until the actual change in corporate ownership took place, only about two weeks were spent exchanging information on computer hardware, systems, applications, communications, or operations, and most of that time was devoted to making an inventory of fixed assets and documenting personnel commitments such as stock options, end of project bonuses, and the like.

My company was one of five acquisitions that had been made within a three-year time period. Except for changing employee benefits and consolidating payroll into the corporate payroll system, little had been done to affect the operations of the earlier four acquisitions. Part of

the reason for this was that the IBM, Digital, Honeywell, and Data General systems of the acquisitions were incompatible with the headquarters Univac operations.

Shortly after we were acquired, I was given the task of consolidating my former company with three of the earlier acquisitions to form what would become initially the largest division in terms of annual revenue. There were three data centers operating mainframes from the same manufacturer, which on paper sounded ideal for achieving some economies of scale. But the three centers had three generations of these mainframes, different versions of the operating systems and system software, multiple peripheral manufacturers, four communications networks involving three different common carriers, and conflicting terms and conditions for purchase and license agreements from the same vendors. There were also redundant accounting, personnel, marketing, and sales staffs.

We began a consolidation study in February 1982 that would take six months and thousands of person hours to complete. In its final reports, the study team—which consisted of staff from all the affected organizations—documented the current situation and recommendations for data centers, computer operations, hardware, software, voice and data communications, staffing, accounting, and marketing and sales—as they would be impacted by the consolidation. For whatever reason, our new parent had neither planned for nor anticipated the millions of dollars in capital and direct expenses it was going to take to implement the consolidation.

It took us 18 months to carry out the consolidation plan. This involved retaining the staff needed to maintain service levels while we expanded one data center and closed down the other two, moved six mainframes and acquired two new ones, renegotiated vendor agreements, merged payroll, personnel, and accounting systems, eliminated redundant functions and operations, and integrated communications networks. When we were finished, we had reduced ongoing operating expenses by almost 20 percent.

We also reduced the preconsolidation workforce by over 52 percent in several stages, including positions lost in a companywide layoff. During the data center closings, we offered outplacement services—including having some potential employers interview on-site—substantial stay bonuses for key employees, relocation assistance, and incentives for nonexempt employees not to abuse accumulated sick leave in order to look for work. There were still a number of early resignations, but our service levels were maintained.

A SHARED EXPERIENCE

Was this experience unique? Based on the results of this study, what we encountered in being acquired and then undertaking a consolidation was consistent with what other companies have reported:

- Acquiring companies focus their attention on salary scales, benefits packages, stock options, accounting conventions, and other issues that impact the bottom line, but they place considerably less emphasis on policies, procedures, and processes;
- In nearly two-thirds of mergers and acquisitions, there is inadequate information shared to make major decisions regarding hardware, software, or voice and data communications systems—and half the time no one thought to ask for the information!
- There is a reduction in the workforce in 3 out of 10 mergers or acquisitions, with no apparent distinction made between exempt and nonexempt staff;
- Health benefits and salary structures change following almost half of the mergers and acquisitions;
- Profitability or payback is the critical success factor for three-quarters of the mergers, acquisitions, and consolidations, but it will take two or more years to measure success properly in over half of them.

AVOIDING THE PROBLEMS CAUSED BY UNCERTAINTY

Communication—or lack thereof—is often the underlying cause of serious problems encountered within 12 months of a merger or acquisition. Understandably, there must be a certain degree of confidentiality in the early stages of discussion about a merger, acquisition, consolidation, or divestiture. But are key members of the human resources and information systems organizations any less trustworthy of this confidence than, say, those in finance, accounting, or marketing? Probably not.

The uncertainty of any organizational change creates ambiguity, which usually results in individuals—and even groups—taking action based on their perceptions of how the change will affect them. There is a need to motivate change, that is, to overcome the natural resistance to entering a newly formed organization and to get people to accept the short-term and long-term goals of the merger, acquisition, consolidation, or divestiture. Where employee dissatisfaction with such a change results from the lack of timely communication from senior management, loss of productivity, lower profitability, high employee turnover, and/or lost market share is twice as likely to result.

Before the proposed organizational change is announced, attention should be paid to how the announcement will be made, what the announcement will contain, how continuing information will be disseminated, who will be the focal point for questions about the change, and so on. Announcement timing itself is critical—nothing can damage employee morale more than to hear first about an organizational change in the news media. It may be feasible to meet with each employee individually or in a group to make the announcement. Whether or not this is possible, a printed announcement should be prepared that covers the following:

- The purpose of the merger, acquisition, consolidation, or divestiture, the schedule for its implementation, the individual(s) who will manage the implementation;
- The short-term impact on the organization—such as any planned changes in benefits, salary scales, staffing, reporting structure, and so forth;
- The conditions under which other changes will be made, including for example the recommendations of any task forces or working groups that may be established;
- How any planned reductions in force will be handled—this requires making decisions up front on job redeployment, early retirement incentives, outplacement services, retraining, stay bonuses, extended severance pay, and other initiatives that might be employed;
- How information about the implementation will be communicated on an ongoing basis, and how individual staff members can get their questions answered.

Participation in organizational change tends to reduce resistance to it. Our own experience is that the formation of working groups to plan the implementation, in detail, of the new organization facilitates the communication of information, helps unearth new information that supports the implementation, and fosters a sense of cooperation among the participants in shaping the longer-term goals of the newly formed organization. Participation does take time and money, and it produces conflicts. This

requires setting a time limit for the working groups and identifying individuals who can manage the organization in transition.

PREPARING INFORMATION SYSTEMS FOR CHANGE

There are a number of things that an information systems department can do to help avoid the potential problems of a future organizational change, such as:

- Having a current systems or technical architecture that documents the information systems environment in terms of hardware, software, communications, operating systems, application development tools, end-user computing support, and so forth;
- Minimizing customization to standard packages for accounting, human resources, payroll, benefit, and purchasing systems;
- Negotiating terms with hardware, software, communications, disaster backup, and other vendors that permit the transfer of rights and obligations to a surviving entity in case of a merger, acquisition, or divestiture.

System changes needed by the newly formed organization will not likely be known ahead of time. Someone in the newly formed organization should be designated as the information systems manager for the transition with the power and authority needed to make the transition happen, working with other information systems managers who are responsible for the ongoing operation. There should be a transition management structure for information systems—task forces or working groups charged with developing system transition plans. Such plans should include the specifications for new or merged systems, implementation milestones, resource requirements, and standards of performance. A parallel activity and plan should be developed for the combined information systems staff.

CONCLUSION

This report identifies some of the problems and issues of forming a new organization following a merger, acquisition, consolidation, or divestiture. The general and specific recommendations suggested here are guidelines that can help minimize or eliminate many of the more common problems by building some stability into the newly formed organization, allowing for participation in the transition planning and implementation, providing communications vehicles for disseminating timely and accurate information, and establishing benchmarks by which the transition can be judged.

Norbert J. Kubilus is vice president for management services at Optimal Solutions, Inc., a New Jersey-based consulting firm that specializes in helping corporations manage change in their information systems organizations. He has held information systems executive positions with Educational Testing Service, National Data Corporation, and Rapidata, Inc., as well as having taught on the graduate faculty of New Jersey Institute of Technology. Mr. Kubilus has been a member of the American Management Association's Information Systems and Technology Council since 1985.

Executive Summary of Statistical Findings

A. Prior to the Merger/Acquisition

1. What information did the acquiring company have in hand prior to the actual acquisition?

Regarding *human resources functions*, respondents had full information on matters impacting the bottom line (i.e., salary scales, benefits packages, stock option plans), only partial information on policy matters (i.e., payroll systems, employment policies and procedures, performance appraisal systems).

Regarding *information systems functions*, fewer than half the respondents had full information on computer hardware systems, and fewer than a third had full information on computer software systems or voice and data communications systems.

Regarding *other management functions*, fewer than half the respondents had full information on budgeting or planning processes, and fewer than a third had full information on purchasing, inventory, delivery, and quality control systems. More than half, however, had full information on accounting conventions and systems, and another 40 percent had information "in part." Only 6.4 percent of respondents found information "not at all available" regarding accounting conventions.

2. Was the available information adequate for major decision making in various functional areas?

Ranging from 74 to 84 percent, respondents agree than the available information *was* adequate for major decision making regarding human resources, benefits and payroll, finance, general management, sales and marketing, and manufacturing. Information was *lacking* regarding information systems, where only 63 percent of respondents agreed that the available information was adequate.

3. Where information was not available, why not?

Because no one thought to ask for it, said 49.5 percent of respondents. 29.4 percent said that lack of information was due to policy considerations; 27.5 percent, because systems were not automated; 14.7 percent, because automated systems couldn't deliver the information.

B. Impact of the Merger/Acquisition on the Human Resources Function in the Newly Formed Organization

1. Did the merger and/or acquisition result in a reduction in force in the newly formed organization?

Over 30 percent of respondents said that the merger and/or acquisition resulted in a reduction in force. The modes: a 10 percent reduction in exempt workers (10 of 33 respondents giving numbers), and 10 percent in nonexempt workers (8 of 26 respondents). The median was 15 percent for both exempts and nonexempts. The highs: 50 percent for exempts (one respondent), 100 percent(!) for nonexempts (one respondent).

2. Was there a revision in health benefits?

Yes, said 45 percent of respondents: 44 percent changed insurance carriers; 22 percent *increased* the corporate contribution per employee for health benefits, while 17 percent lowered the corporate contribution; 19 percent *increased* the employee contribution for health benefits, while 11 percent decreased the employee contribution.

3. Was the salary structure revised?

Yes: 20.2 percent of respondents *increased* the number of pay levels for exempt workers, while 23.9 percent *decreased* the number of exempt pay levels; 11.9 percent increased the number of pay levels for nonexempts, while 14.7 percent decreased the number of nonexempt pay levels.

4. Scales for statements on the effect of the merger/acquisition on the newly formed organization.

In all cases, responses ranged widely from *7*, indicating strong agreement with the statement, to *1*, indicating strong disagreement.

a. "Employees in both the acquired and parent companies were kept informed on developments and changes associated with the merger/ acquisition." Mode: 5 (26.6 percent). Ave: 3.66.

b. "The human resources function in the parent and/or the acquired company played an important role in premerger or acquisition planning." Mode: 1 (24.3 percent). Ave: 3.18.

c. "Changes in staff and in policies and procedures had a serious negative impact on employee morale." Modes: 1, 2, and 3 each at 18.7 percent. Ave: 3.49.

d. "The following factors contributed strongly to employee dissatisfaction:"

    i. "Lack of timely communication from senior management." Mode: 1 (18.9 percent), but note 17.8 percent at *6*. Ave.: 3.73.

    ii. "Discrepancies in salary and benefits programs." Mode: 1 (26.2 percent), but note 21.5 percent at *4*. Ave: 3.07.

    iii. "Workforce reductions." Mode: 1 (22.4 percent), but note 21.5 percent at *4*. Ave: 3.46.

    iv. "Changes in staff, policies, and systems." Mode: 4 (20.6 percent). Ave: 3.74.

    v. "Management turnover." Mode: 5 (22.4 percent), but note 19.6 percent at *1*. Ave: 3.58.

e. "The merger/acquisition resulted in an important change in the organization's management structure." Mode: 7(!) (27.1 percent). Ave: 4.92.

5. If there was an important change in the

management structure, what was the nature of the change?

24.7 percent of respondents cited "fewer layers of management." 33.9 percent cited "greater centralization of key functions," while 13.8 percent said the opposite: "decentralization of key functions."

6. *In determining which people would remain with the newly formed organization and which would be discharged, which of these policies did you follow?*

26.6 percent automatically retained all employees wishing to stay; 21 percent automatically eliminated redundant positions. 44.3 percent carried out one-on-one interviews to determine individual talent and capability. 36.7 percent retained individuals who met specific criteria.

7. *In eliminating redundant positions, what were decisions based upon?*

16.5 percent of respondents based such decisions on previous service with the *parent* company; 24.8 percent on previous service with the *acquired* company. 26.6 percent based the decision on length of service; 49.5 percent on past performance. Ten percent used other criteria.

C. **Impact of the Merger/Acquisition on the MIS Function in the Newly Formed Organization**

1. *In which functions did system incompatibility prove a problem?*

Incompatibility proved a problem for a range of 17 to 31 percent of respondents, depending on the function: at the high end were general ledger (31.2 percent), general and administrative (30.3 percent), and accounts payable/receivable (27.5 percent);

at the low end, production and distribution (17.8 percent of manufacturing companies), and purchasing (19.3 percent).

2. *What priorities were established in merging systems?*

Financial systems had highest priority among 40.4 percent of respondents. HR systems had lowest priority among 24.8 percent. A rough ranking by modal response:

> Financial: 40.4 percent ranked at 1
> Operational: 31.2 percent ranked at 2
> Human Resources: 19.3 percent ranked at 3
> Payroll: 21.4 percent ranked at 4
> Benefits: 24.8 percent ranked at 5 (likewise HR)
> Other: 56.9 percent ranked at 6

3. *How much time was spent merging systems?*

Just under half the respondents (45.9 percent) had systems merged within six months of the merger/acquisition. An additional 22.9 percent had systems merged within a year.

4. *Was a service bureau used to handle some data processing due to limited or strained MIS capacity?*

Yes, by 14.7 percent of respondents. An additional 17.4 percent considered using a service bureau but decided against it. 36.7 percent of respondents would consider using a service bureau in the future.

5. *What MIS expenditures were directly attributable to the merger/acquisition?*

a. *Hardware.* 14.7 percent of respondents made computer hardware expenditures attributable to the merger/acquisition. One respondent spent as little as $5,000; another, as much as $500,000. Half spent $50,000 or less; half spent $75,000 or more on hardware.

b. *Software*. 17.4 percent of respondents made computer software expenditures attributable to the merger/acquisition. One respondent spent as little as $1,200; another, as much as $500,000. Half spent $25,000 or less; half spent $40,000 or more on software.

c. *Training of non-MIS personnel*. 13.8 percent of respondents had training expenditures directly attributable to the merger/acquisition. One spent as little as $3,000; another, as much as $300,000. Half spent $10,000 or less; half spent $25,000 or more on training.

D. Gauging the Results of Mergers and Acquisitions

1. What problems were encountered in the 12 months following the merger/acquisition?

24.7 percent of respondents reported a loss in worker productivity; 14.7 percent, a loss of market share; 24.8 percent, lesser profitability; 35.8 percent, high employee turnover.

2. What are the best ways to determine the success of an acquisition or merger?

Profitability was the most important measure, according to 39.8 percent of respondents; payback, according to 36.1 percent; market share, according to 10.2 percent. Among "other" criteria listed by respondents were shareholder value improvement; technology and products; return on investment; long-term growth; cash flow to reduce debt; and workforce security.

3. How long a time must pass before success can be properly measured?

The modal response from 29.6 percent of respondents was two to three years, closely followed by three to five years (28.7 percent), and one to two years (27.8 percent).

1

The New Reality

Mergers and acquisitions impose a new reality upon organizations. Often they enable companies to streamline business activities, but frequently they create many problems that result in lesser productivity, market share, and profits.

So began a four-page American Management Association questionnaire mailed in the spring of 1988 to selected companies recently engaged in mergers and acquisitions. Its emphasis: the impact of the merger or acquisition on the newly formed organization's human resources and information systems functions.

The questionnaire, designed with the help of Control Data Business Management Services and the accounting firm of Peat, Marwick and Main, drew 109 responses. The data from the questionnaire's four areas of inquiry shed statistical light on the degree to which problems were anticipated, and the measures respondent firms took to deal with such problems.

But statistics were only the beginning. Extended telephone interviews with two-thirds of the respondents yielded specific insights into the manner in which acquiring firms brought merger targets into the fold. The Grow Group, a New York-based chemical firm that has been particularly active in acquisitions and mergers, shared with us its own information checklist for target companies. Members of various

AMA Councils were sounded for additional information; Norbert J. Kubilis, vice president for management services at Optimal Solutions and a member of AMA's Information Systems and Technology Council, wrote the foreword that begins this report.

Every survey must balance the breadth of its statistical sample against the depth of the information it seeks. Various sources estimate the number of companies involved in mergers and acquisitions at anywhere from 3,500 to 7,500 annually. The AMA sample for this report (see Table 1) is *not* a scientifically selected cross-section of such companies. Statistically, a sample of this size contains a margin of error of 9.5 percent (which means that if the same questions were asked of 109 different companies, the statistics would vary by as much as 9.5 percent on each question).

Our intention, then, was not to develop benchmark statistics for all the mergers and acquisitions that have taken place in recent years. The breadth of the sample was not our first concern. We were aware that a majority of com-

Table 1. The AMA sample—mergers and acquisitions survey.

| | | | Annual Sales | | | | | |
	-$100M		$100–$500M		+$500M		Total	
Manufacturers	16	25.0%	13	76.5%	16	57.1%	45	41.0%
Service providers	41	64.1	4	23.5	10	35.7	55	50.0
Other	7	10.9	0	0.0	2	7.1	9	8.0
Total	64	58.7	17	15.6	28	25.7	109	100.0

panies acquired in the 1980s were small ones, many with ill-defined or nonexistent human resources or IST departments.

What we sought instead was information *in depth* about the specific functional areas of human resources and information management. We made no inquiries about how target companies were identified, or about any of the purely financial or market data that acquiring companies seek. We did not ask if takeovers were friendly or hostile. We focused, as AMA research does, on the *management* issues: how companies deal with the new realities in human resources and in information systems in the aftermath of a merger or acquisition.

WHAT WE ASKED

The AMA questionnaire featured four fields of inquiry:

- What information was available to the acquiring or parent company prior to the acquisition or merger?
- What impact did the acquisition or merger have on the *human resources* function in the newly formed organization?
- What impact did the acquisition or merger have on the *management information system* in the newly formed organization?
- What were the tangible results of the acquisition or merger in the 12 months

following the event? How is success best measured?

In each field, respondents were asked to make qualitative judgments. Such judgments are inherently subjective. But where appropriate, we also asked for quantitative data—hard numbers on workforce reductions where they occurred, or on the costs of merging informations systems. And while we did not ask for specific figures in the final section of the questionnaire ("Gauging the Results of Mergers and Acquisitions"), we listed four problem areas that can be quantified:

- Loss in worker productivity
- Loss of market share
- Lesser profitability
- High employee turnover

Problems, Problems . . .

"When sorrows come," wrote Shakespeare, "they come not in single espials, but in battalions." Eight respondent firms reported that they suffered all four of the postevent problems listed in the questionnaire. The problem most prevalent was high employee turnover; least reported was loss of market share. Table 2 lists the figures in full.

In all, half of our respondent companies reported that they encountered one or more of these problems in the 12 months following the acquisition or merger. This statistical fact allowed us to make a series of comparisons in all

Table 2. Postevent problems cited by 54 survey respondents.

	Only problem reported (22)	1 of 2 problems reported (17)	1 of 3 problems reported (7)	1 of 4 problems reported (8)	Total reporting problem
Loss in worker productivity	6	9	4	8	27
Loss of market share	2	3	3	8	16
Lesser profitability	2	10	7	8	27
High employee turnover	12	12	7	8	39

of our areas of inquiry. Did the 54 respondents who encountered postmerger/acquisition problems approach the event and manage it in an importantly different manner from the 55 respondents who reported no such problems?

SUMMARY OF FINDINGS

Some brief answers:

- Postevent workforce reductions correlate highly with postevent problems. Of the 36 firms that initiated workforce reductions after the merger or acquisition, 69 percent encountered one or more of the problems listed above; of the 73 firms that did not reduce their workforces, 40 percent encountered such problems.
- Companies that automatically eliminated redundant positions were twice as likely to report postevent problems as those that followed other policies in deciding who would stay and who would go in the wake of a merger or acquisition.
- Attempts to centralize key management functions also signaled problems. One-

third of the respondent companies told us they'd altered the management structure of the organization in the direction of greater centralization; of these 37 firms, 23, or 62 percent, reported postevent problems. Of the remaining 72 companies, only 43 percent cited such problems.

- In the same regard, changes in staff and in policies and procedures had a negative impact on employee morale in the majority of companies reporting postevent problems. This was not the case among "problem-free" respondents.
- Companies that had to deal with incompatibility of information systems, especially in such functions as human resources, general administration, purchasing, and production and distribution, reported a far higher incidence of the problems listed above than did firms reporting no such incompatibilities. Moreover, respondents that moved quickly to resolve their incompatibility problems found themselves with fewer postevent problems.
- Companies that decreased corporate contributions to employee health plans in the wake of a merger or acquisition were far more likely to encounter prob-

lems than those that maintained or increased such contributions. Two-thirds of the 19 respondents who decreased corporate contributions reported one or more of the postevent problems listed, compared with fewer than half of all others.

AMA research focused entirely on the *internal* workings of the newly formed organization. Certainly, external forces may play an equal or even larger role in determining the eventual success of corporate buyouts or weddings. But companies cannot control such external forces. They can only manage themselves—and in so doing, better prepare themselves for the inevitable and unavoidable stresses they will encounter when companies meet and marry.

2

Prior to the Merger or Acquisition

Clearly, internal policies and systems do not play a determining role when companies consider an acquisition or merger. Yet, when the deal is done, these are the facts of worklife that confront the new management.

WAS INFORMATION AVAILABLE?

For this reason, the AMA questionnaire began with a probe on what the acquiring or parent company knew about various management functions in the target organization in advance of the merger or acquisition. We asked:

> What information did the acquiring company have in hand prior to the actual acquisition?

We organized three lists. The first focused on human resources and payroll functions; the second, on information systems functions; the third, on general management functions. In each case, we asked if information was available in full, in part, or not at all.

A summary of our findings:

- Regarding *human resources functions* (see Figure 1), respondents had full information on matters impacting the bottom line (i.e., salary scales, benefits packages, stock option plans), only partial information on policy matters (i.e., payroll systems, employment policies and procedures, performance appraisal systems). Put another way, respondents gathered more information on matters touching senior management than on policies affecting supervisory and hourly employees.
- Regarding *information systems functions* (see Figure 2), fewer than half the respondents had full information on computer hardware systems, and fewer than a third had full information on computer software systems or voice and data communications systems.
- Regarding *other management functions* (see Figure 3), fewer than half the respondents had full information on budgeting or planning processes, and fewer

Figure 1. Understanding the human resources/payroll functions.

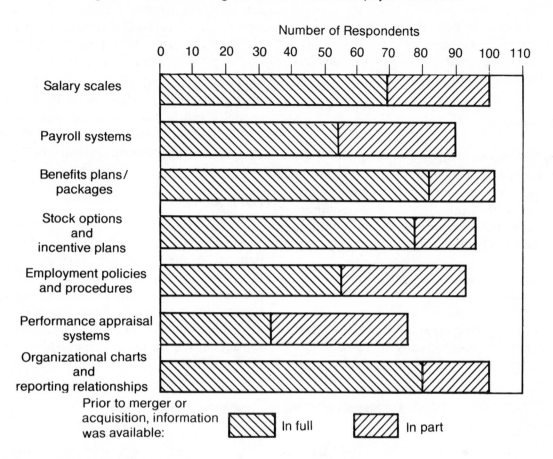

than a third had full information on purchasing, inventory, delivery, and quality control systems. More than half, however, had full information on accounting conventions and systems, and another 40 percent had information "in part." Only 6.4 percent of respondents found information "not at all available" regarding accounting conventions.

Money matters are primary, policy matters secondary when companies gather information on target firms. This is an all but universal priority, observed in equal regard by respondents that reported postevent problems and by respondents reporting no such problems.

WAS INFORMATION ADEQUATE?

Although available in various degrees, information on business functions might or might not provide an adequate basis for decision making. We listed seven prime business functions, and asked:

> Was the available information adequate for major decision making in various functional areas?

The findings, in brief:

■ By majorities ranging from 74 to 84 percent, respondents agreed than the available information *was* adequate for major decision making regarding human resources, benefits and payroll, finance, general management, sales and marketing, and manufacturing. (See Figure 4; note that the bar labeled "Manufacturing" gives the percentage of 45 manufacturers in the sample that agree with the statement.)

■ Information was *lacking* regarding information systems, where only 63 percent of respondents said that the available information was adequate.

If Not, Why Not?

Where information (particularly computerized information) is not available, there may be a technological problem: records may not be automated or, if they are, they may prove impossible to transfer from one system to another. We therefore asked:

> Where information was not available, why not?

But people, not machines, were at the root of the problem. A near majority of respondents (49.5 percent) told us that information was not available simply because no one thought to ask for it. Thirty percent said that lack of information was due to policy considerations—a euphemism, perhaps, for a hostile environment.

Technology played a lesser role: 27.5 percent of respondents said that information could not be delivered because systems were not automated, and 14.7 percent told us that automated systems couldn't deliver the information.

Did It Matter?

We compared statistics from the 54 respondents who cited postevent problems with figures from the 55 who came through the event problem-free and found that the amount or quality of information on systems and policies available to the parent company had little or no impact on the eventual success of the merger or acquisition.

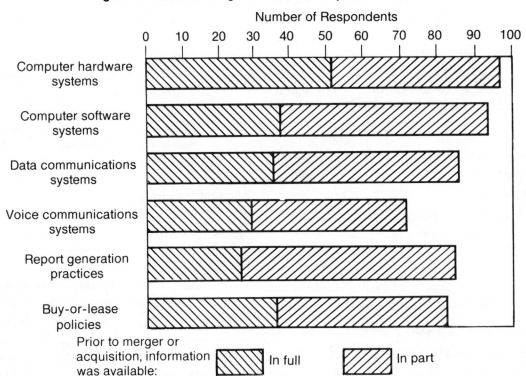

Figure 2. Understanding the information systems function.

Figure 3. Understanding budget, accounting, and other functional systems.

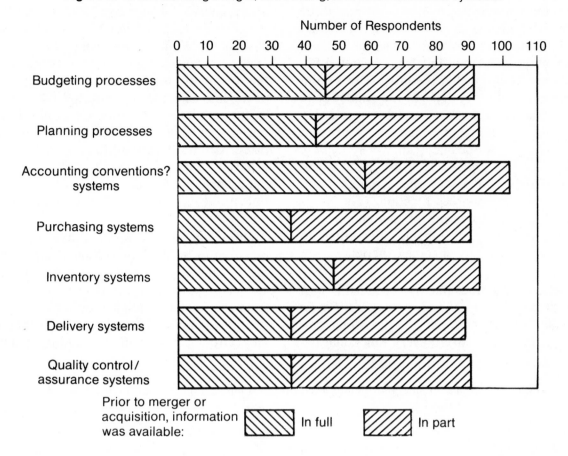

What mattered was how the new organization moved to change or rationalize the incompatibilities that did exist. That was the subject of the questionnaire's further sections.

GROW GROUP: A LESSON IN DUE DILIGENCE

One company, Grow Group, has taken a highly organized approach to preacquisition information gathering. For Grow Group, such information is vital to assessment and financial planning. Most important, its "due diligence" list ferrets out potential problems and is an enormous time saver.

Over the past half-century, Grow Group, Inc., has evolved from a small supplier of solvents and speciality thinners for auto makers to a publicly owned corporation with annual sales in excess of half a billion dollars (before divestiture of its health and beauty aids subsidiary). Its core business remains the production of paints and chemical coatings for architectural, marine, transportation, and other industrial products. Through acquisitions and joint ventures, it has entered a variety of other fields, among them health and beauty aids, household and industrial cleaning and maintenance products, swimming pool and spa chemicals. Its president and chief executive officer, Russell Banks, serves on the American Management Association's General Management Council.

Teresa McCaslin, Grow Group's vice president of human resources, explained to AMA researchers how the due diligence concept came about. For Grow Group, merger and acquisition activity has accelerated over the past three years. This increased activity brought to Mc-Caslin's attention redundancies in the kinds of information she requested from potential acquisitions. Additionally, the process was painfully piecemeal for both parties, with McCaslin calling the target company at least once a day to request additional information. As a result, she developed a document known as *Human Resources Due Diligence*, a list of all documents needed to assess the acquired company's human resources function. (The list is printed in full at the end of this chapter.) It became a "living document," according to McCaslin, created by ongoing experience.

The human resources due diligence list is part of a 20–page *Comprehensive Checklist for an Acquisition* (see Appendix). This all-encompassing document covers every functional de-

partment in a target firm. Yet all the lists are interrelated to some degree. "When we sat down to develop the human resources list we thought of all the paperwork we needed to analyze, and we asked other departments in the company what information they would need. For example, legal would be interested in any pending EEO suits that would become our responsibility after the acquisition took place. Or the financial group would be interested in the pension plan, in order to evaluate the company's liability at the time of acquisition."

Additionally, outside vendors played an important role in the list's development. For example, in one case, Grow Group's major medical carrier requested a three-year risk analysis from the potential acquisition's carrier. From this information, the insurer would then provide Grow Group with a reasonable assess-

Figure 4. Was available information adequate for major decision making in these areas?

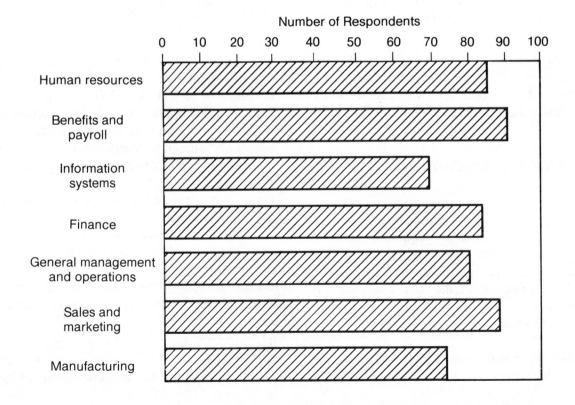

ment of their premium risk after the acquisition.

Due Diligence Advantage

What is the advantage of the due diligence list? According to McCaslin, it provides an organized format for company assessment on two fronts. First, it provides the acquirer with all the policies and procedures needed for a compatibility assessment. Second, it provides the numbers for costing out the benefit plans and policies of the population group involved in the takeover, as well as for those who could be terminated as a result of the merger or acquisition.

The list is a major time saver, says McCaslin. "Instead of calling the company on a daily basis, asking for documents in a piecemeal fashion, we can hand them, fax them, or mail them this list—and then they can compile all the information in an organized fashion."

Additionally, it prevents documentation from slipping through the cracks. "If you ask for their pension plan, for example, you might get only the original—without subsequent amendments or revisions," explains McCaslin. "Although human resources staffs work with their plans every day, it's easy to overlook changes. This list provides a trigger for memory."

Red Light, Green Light . . .

Once in hand, the documentation is reviewed over a 10–day to two-week period. This evaluation is an integral part of the decision-making process, with the entire company's portfolio laid bare. "Based on our findings at the time, we will either proceed with the acquisition, or uncover so many problems that we drop the offer," says McCaslin.

The review does uncover potential problems that can be worked on during the planning phase. When acquisition plans are dropped, the decision usually comes from the financial group or the environmental committee, rarely from HR, where experience has shown that most problems can be ironed out.

But there are instances when a red light flashes in human resources. The pension plan, according to McCaslin, is one such area. Pension liability—and the potential drainage of excess assets—can make the acquisition questionable. Additionally, incompatible policies may create insurmountable problems. For example, the new company may segment its population and treat each segment differently, whereas Grow Group tends to treat all its employees equally—except for unionized companies when bargaining is necessary (pension, disability, and major medical), perhaps as a result of the new company's own acquisitions.

According to McCaslin, due diligence is a prime asset in the planning phase, but it can, and does, extend further. She pointed out that many of the legal documents can be spun off the volumes of books that are put together for this evaluation.

And Behind Door Number Two . . .

There have been no major surprises related to human resources in Grow Group's acquisitions, and McCaslin attributes this to the list and the brainstorming behind it. "Our environmental group hasn't found major toxic waste dumps after the acquisition. Catastrophic medical claims haven't surfaced once I've asked for experience rates from major medical carriers. These problems would have come up in the beginning, and we would have worked them out during the planning phase."

Most of Grow Group's acquisitions have been relatively problem-free—primarily because the company does not participate in hostile takeovers. But there is always a period of adjustment. "People are working for a different company, with a different style," McCaslin cautions. "In some cases our benefits are better, but sometimes, especially when we've acquired a small part of a larger company, they're not. Employees aren't quite as happy then, but adjustment usually comes."

This adjustment usually occurs from the top down. Grow Group initially sets up contact with senior management, to get them to sign on to the changes. With the employee population, communication tends to be a little more structured. "Ideally, we like the departing organization to make a presentation, explaining to the employees what they will be *getting* as a result of the divestiture," explains McCaslin. "Then we come in immediately, conducting employee meetings day and night—giving them information about the company and about the benefit plans. Also, we try to enroll them into our plans at that time." Additionally, Grow Group makes efforts to reach its Spanish-speaking employee segments by providing needed information bilingually. "The important part is to keep communicating, especially at the beginning," asserts McCaslin. "People don't like change. The more hand holding you do in the beginning, the better the transition."

There tends to be some fallout among employees—McCaslin estimates turnover at about 20 percent over the first two years. But the turnover is not so much among senior managers as middle and lower management teams. "What we mostly hear," says McCaslin, "is that they'd like to go back to the original company, or that too much is changing around them, or that they don't like the way their positions are evolving. With senior management, if you give them responsibilities equal to or greater than they had previously, and they believe the op-

portunity for growth is there, they tend to be self-motivated."

CULTURE CLASH

Not all acquisitions are problem-free, and not all problems surface in the planning phase. According to McCaslin, it is important to examine the two companies' corporate cultures. When they are diametrically opposed, postacquisition problems mount.

Culture conflicts can arise in various forms:

- East versus West: what happens when button-down, pinstripe management from the East Coast acquires a laid-back, surf's-up California business? The IBM-Rolm deal is a primary example.
- Big fish versus little fish: the target business may be a small division of its original parent; when acquired, it may find itself among the larger operating units of the newly formed organization. Or, conversely, a one-time whale may suddenly feel itself a minnow in a megacorporation.
- Centralization versus decentralization: a highly centralized original parent may sell a piece of its business to a management group that adopts a hands-off attitude. Lacking daily instruction, the acquired business may lose direction.

For itself, Grow Group allows its acquired business a very wide degree of latitude. "We have a very small corporate headquarters," McCaslin explains, "and when we acquire a company we are as interested in its management and staff as we are in the product. We don't look to consolidate operations."

Due Diligence Human Resources Checklist for Mergers and Acquisitions

I. *Policies and Procedures*
1. Copy of personnel policies and procedures manual
2. Copy of employee handbook(s)
3. Copies of all existing employment contracts
4. Copies of all existing "golden," "silver," "tin" parachute agreements and changes in company control severance agreements

II. *General Personnel*
1. Complete set of organization charts (account for each employee)
2. Lines of succession—backing of key positions
3. Employee headcount (by function and location), list of employees by name, title, date of hire, date of employment, FLSB status (exempt, nonexempt, etc.) by department. Preferably include complete personnel file for each employee
4. List of directors, officers, committees, and their duties
5. Biographical information for key senior managers, including age, years with company, and employment history
6. Copy of position description for key management employees
7. List of potential voluntary resignations of key management if merged/acquired
8. Review of adequacy of office staff by department
9. Check of physical arrangement or adequacy of offices

III. *Compensation*
1. Summary compensation administration (increases, evaluations, etc.) for three employee groups: exempt, nonexempt salaried, hourly nonunion
2. Rating and evaluation of all personnel with managerial responsibilities
3. Copies of incentive compensation plans, bonus plans, productivity improvement plans

IV. *Employee Benefits*
1. Summary plan descriptions of all benefit plans
   A. 401 (K)
   B. Major medical/hospitalization
   C. Profit sharing
   D. Pension
   E. Life insurance
2. Copies of whole life split dollar insurance policies
3. Descriptions of any other benefits such as
   A. Service awards
   B. Short-term absences
   C. Relocation
   D. Vacations/holiday schedules
   E. PAYSOP/LESOP/KSOP
4. Three-year experience rate for major medical expenses paid/incurred
5. Three-year experience rate for life insurance paid/incurred
6. Monthly insured plan cost for salaried and hourly personnel to include COBRA extension costs

7. Copy of stock option plan; list of all employees with options, dates of grant(s), number of shares, option price, exercisable amounts
8. Employee purchase programs
9. List of special executive perquisites, qualifers, and list of participating executives
10. Key employee insurance programs

V. *Worker's Compensation*
1. Summary outlining all Worker's Compensation claims pending
2. Worker's Compensation experience rate during past four-year period

VI. *Employee Relations*
1. List of all pending EEO suits, grievances, arbitrations, and private employee litigation
2. Three-year experience history for EEO suits, arbitrations, legal suits
3. Status of compliance with immigration law effective November 6, 1987
4. List of all employees currently on short-term or long-term disability; date of disability; date of expected return; reason for disability

VII. *Labor Relations*
1. Copies of all existing union contracts
2. Copies of published work rules and regulations
3. Past key difficulties with existing union
4. Present labor situation and working relationships
5. Pending problems, if any
6. Methods of hiring and discharging
7. Job classifications and rates
8. Methods of payment
9. Working conditions
10. Morale and productivity

VIII. *Outside Consultants/Temporary Services*
1. List of consultants and outside services used, including fee arrangements
2. Review of special hiring practices (i.e., covering peak production periods; use of temporaries, contract employees, etc.)

3

Managing the Transition

Matthew Arnold wrote, "Change doth unknit the tranquil strength of men." In the best of all possible worlds, a well-managed transition takes enormous skill on the part of planners. On the other hand, a worst case scenario can mean a disgruntled workforce, financial loss, and more problems than anyone could have anticipated. What was the fallout for companies that encountered problems? And what did those that were problem-free do right that the others didn't do?

IMPACT: THE HUMAN RESOURCES FUNCTION

Human resources managers, though infrequently involved in premerger or preacquisition planning (as we shall see), are often the first to deal with the new postevent reality: reductions in force, altered benefit packages, and revised salary structures are common examples.

How frequently did such changes accompany a merger or acquisition, and in what degree?

These are the questions we posed. The first asked:

> Did the merger and/or acquisition result in a reduction in force in the newly formed organization?

Thirty-six percent of respondents said that the event resulted in a reduction in force. (See Figure 5 for reductions in nonexempt workers, Figure 6 for reductions in hourly workers.) The modes: a 10 percent reduction in exempt workers (10 of 33 respondents giving numbers), and 10 percent in nonexempt workers (8 of 26 respondents). The median was 15 percent for both exempts and nonexempts. The highs: 50 percent for exempts (2 respondents), 100 percent(!) for nonexempts (one respondent).

The negative effects of workforce reductions were dramatic. Seventy percent of the companies that downsized in the wake of the merger or acquisition reported one or more postevent problems, compared with 40 percent of companies that retained all their workers. And the greater the layoffs, the greater the incidence of

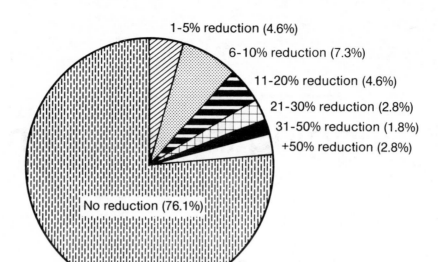

Figure 5. Reductions in force following the merger or acquisition: hourly workers.

1-5% reduction (4.6%)

6-10% reduction (7.3%)

11-20% reduction (4.6%)

21-30% reduction (2.8%)

31-50% reduction (1.8%)

+50% reduction (2.8%)

No reduction (76.1%)

postevent problems: 17 of the 20 companies that lopped off more than 10 percent of their exempt or nonexempt workers reported postevent problems. (See Tables 3 and 4.)

What relationships existed between workforce reductions and specific postevent problems? Table 5 shows that companies that reduced workforces were half again as likely to find their profits reduced, almost twice as likely to experience high employee turnover, and nearly three times as likely to suffer losses in worker productivity and in market share.

It is tempting, but unwise, to conclude that in a merger or acquisition, workforce reductions should be avoided at all costs. Inevitable redundancies must be eliminated, and staffing must be rationalized. As seen above, 40 percent of companies that avoided workforce reductions nevertheless reported postevent problems. But senior managers must understand that there will be a price to pay.

Decisions on Personnel

That price can be affected, at least in part, by policy choices. The questionnaire asked:

> In determining which people would remain with the newly formed organization and which would be discharged, which of these policies did you follow?

Figure 7 gives the policy options listed in the questionnaire, and displays the number of respondents using each, either alone or in combination with others.

One of these—the automatic elimination of redundant positions—correlates highly with the report of postevent problems. Two-thirds of the firms that automatically eliminated personnel redundancies encountered one or more of the problems listed, compared with one-third of all others. The other policies show no such correlation.

Companies that must eliminate redundant personnel may choose among various criteria. Table 6 lists the options presented in the questionnaire.

Again, one (and only one) option correlates highly with postevent problems. Twenty of the 29 firms that used length of service as a basis of decision, or 69 percent, experienced one or more of the problems cited. Because length of service is the only purely quantitative measure among the four listed in Table 6, the finding suggests that there is no easy way out of a very delicate situation; those who are counting years of service to determine who shall stay and who shall go, rather than making more qualitative judgments, are suffering the consequences.

Management Structure

Nearly three-quarters of the survey respondents reported that the merger or acquisition resulted in an important change in the organization's management structure. The most frequent change—a shift toward greater centralization of key functions—also signaled a higher incidence of postevent problems.

The questionnaire asked:

> If there was an important change in the management structure, what was the nature of the change?

Table 7 displays the results.

Of the 79 companies that reported some type of change in management structure, 47, or 59.5 percent, also reported postevent problems; of the 30 others, only 7, or 23.3 percent, reported such problems. By definition, change upsets the status quo, inevitably and—in many instances—necessarily. But of all potential changes, centralization apparently produces the greatest *cumulative* impact on the newly formed organization.

We term the impact "cumulative" for this reason: companies that centralized key management functions did not report any one *particular* postmerger problem more frequently than did the others. Rather, they reported a greater *incidence* of problems across the board. Companies that centralized reported a total of 44 incidents of postevent problems, compared

Figure 6. Reductions in force after the merger or acquisition: managers, technicians, and professionals.

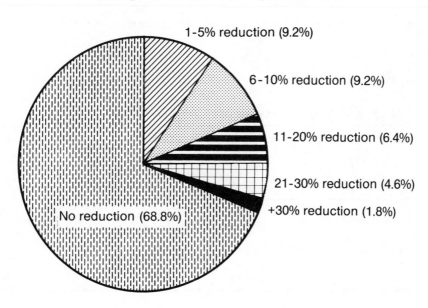

Table 3. Incidence of postevent problems as an effect of workforce reductions among managers, technicians, and professionals.

Pct. of nonexempt workers discharged	Number of companies	Number/Pct. reporting postevent problems		Number/Pct. reporting no such problems	
0%	75	31	41.3%	44	58.7%
1–5	10	5	50.0	5	50.0
6–10	10	7	70.0	3	30.0
11–20	7	5	71.4	2	28.6
21–30	5	4	80.0	1	20.0
+30	2	2	100.0	0	0.0

Table 4. Incidence of postevent problems as an effect of workforce reductions among hourly workers.

Pct. of hourly workers discharged	Number of companies	Number/Pct. reporting postevent problems		Number/Pct. reporting no such problems	
0%	83	34	41.0%	49	59.0%
1–5	5	3	60.0	2	40.0
6–10	8	5	62.5	3	37.5
11–20	5	5	100.0	0	0.0
21–30	3	3	100.0	0	0.0
31–50	2	1	50.0	1	50.0
+50	3	3	100.0	0	0.0

Table 5. Correlation of workforce reductions to postevent problems.

Postevent problem reported	36 companies reducing workforce		73 companies not reducing workforce	
	#	%	#	%
Loss in worker productivity	15	41.7	12	16.4
Loss of market share	9	25.0	7	9.6
Lesser profitability	12	33.3	15	20.5
High employee turnover	19	52.8	20	27.4
Any of the above	25	69.4	29	39.7

Figure 7. Policies used to determine employee retention after the merger or acquisition.

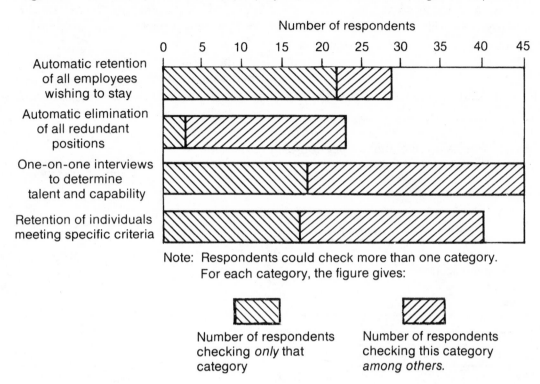

Note: Respondents could check more than one category. For each category, the figure gives:

Number of respondents checking *only* that category

Number of respondents checking this category *among others.*

with 19 incidents among companies that decentralized, and 29 incidents among companies that "flattened" their organizations by eliminating layers of management.

Conversely, the 30 companies that made no important changes in management structure had by far the least incidence of postmerger problems. Table 8 makes the point.

Salary Structure

The questionnaire asked whether organizational salary structures had been revised, and if so, whether the revision had resulted in an increase or decrease in the number of pay levels for exempts and/or for nonexempts.

For 47 respondents, the answer was yes. Managerial salary structures were subject to adjustment far more frequently than were those for nonexempts; revisions were as likely to in-

crease the number of pay levels as to decrease them. Twenty percent of respondents increased the number of pay levels for exempt workers, while 24 percent decreased them; 12 percent increased the number of pay levels for nonexempts, while 15 percent decreased them.

There were no statistical correlations between adjustments in salary structures and postevent problems, nor did such adjustments have any measurable impact on employee morale. Their effect on systems integration will be addressed further on in this report.

Benefits

Did the merger or acquisition result in a revision in the structure of health benefits? Yes, said 45 percent of survey respondents. And the revision almost always involved a change in insurance carriers. Of the 49 companies that altered their health plans, 48 reported a change in carriers.

More often than not, a revision in health benefits involved an increase in premiums, whether for the employer or the employee. But decreased premiums were by no means rare. (See Table 9.)

Of the 19 firms that decreased corporate contributions to health plans, 13, or 68 percent, reported postevent problems; of all others, 45.5 percent reported such problems.

Another statistical finding, more fully developed below, underscores the potential negative impact when health benefits costs are shifted

Table 6. Basis of decision to eliminate personnel in redundant positions.

	Number of respondents	
	Only basis used	Used in combination with others
Previous service with parent company	0	18
Previous service with acquired company	0	27
Length of service	1	28
Past performance	22	32

Table 7. Nature of postevent changes in management structure.

	Companies reporting postevent problems	Companies reporting no such problems	All
Fewer layers of management	27.8%	21.8%	24.8
Greater centralization of key functions	42.6	25.5	33.9
Decentralization of key functions	16.7	10.9	13.8
No important change	13.0	41.8	27.5

Table 8. Correlation of changes in management structure to incidence of postevent problems.

	Reporting loss in worker productivity	Reporting loss of market share	Reporting lesser profit-ability	Reporting high employee turnover
Greater centralization of key functions (37)	29.7%	18.9%	24.3%	45.9%
Fewer layers of management (27)	25.9	11.1	25.9	44.4
Decentralization of key functions (15)	26.7	20.0	46.7	33.3
No important change (30)	16.7	10.0	13.3	16.7

Table 9. Postevent changes in contributions to health plans.

	Percent reporting increase	Percent reporting decrease	Percent reporting no change
Corporate contribution	22.0	17.4	60.6
Employee contribution	19.3	11.0	69.7

onto the shoulders of the employees. As will be seen, the AMA questionnaire posed a series of statements about employee morale, and provided a 7-to-1 scale for responses, a 7 indicating strong agreement with the statement, a 1, strong disagreement. Among those statements: *"Changes in staff and in policies and procedures had a serious negative impact on employee morale."*

Five firms in the sample *decreased* corporate contributions to health plans and *increased* employee contributions. Responding to the statement above, these five companies produced an average of 5.80 on the 7-point scale—a very high measure of agreement. Conversely, three firms *increased* corporate contributions and *decreased* employee premiums. Among these three companies, the response averaged 2.67—announcing strong *disagreement* that the changes had a negative impact. Simply put, health care revisions that hike employee contributions produce a high measure of ill feeling among those employees.

Upsetting the Applecart

The remark is ascribed to Calvin Coolidge: "When people are thrown out of work, unemployment results." And why shouldn't the late President say so? He had the statistics to back up the claim.

The AMA survey produced a clutch of statistical correlations that simply confirm what most managers intuitively feel: that organizations perform better when they practice good top-down communication, sensitivity in employee relations, and continuity in staffing and policies. Respondent firms that ignored these obvious points reaped the consequences—losses in worker productivity, lesser profits, and high employee turnover.

The AMA questionnaire read:

> Here are a series of statements on the effect of the merger or acquisition on the newly formed company. Each statement is accompanied by a 7–to–1 scale. We ask you . . . to indicate the extent to which you agree or disagree with the statement. A 7 would indicate strong agreement; a 1, strong disagreement.
>
> A. Employees in both the acquired and parent companies were kept informed on developments and changes associated with the merger/acquisition.
>
> B. The human resources function in the parent and/or the acquired company played an important role in premerger (or acquisition) planning.
>
> C. Changes in staff and in policies and procedures had a serious negative impact on employee morale.

Tables 10, 11, and 12 display the data. To summarize the findings: keeping employees informed on developments gives companies a slight but measurable edge in avoiding postevent problems; involving human resources managers in premerger planning increases that

Table 10. "Employees in both the acquired and parent companies were kept informed on developments and changes associated with the merger/acquisition."

	Companies reporting postevent problems	Companies reporting no such problems	All
Average on 7-point scale	3.35	3.84	3.66
Mode on 7-point scale	5	5	5
Agreed with statement (5, 6 or 7 on scale)	35.2%	47.3%	41.3%
Disagreed with statement (1, 2, or 3 on scale)	50.0%	41.8%	45.9%
Neutral (4 on scale)	14.8%	10.9%	12.8%

Table 11. "The human resources function in the parent and/or acquired company played an important role in premerger or preacquisition planning."

	Companies reporting postevent problems	Companies reporting no such problems	All
Average on 7-point scale	2.96	3.27	3.18
Mode on 7-point scale	1 & 3	4	1
Agreed with statement (5, 6 or 7 on scale)	18.5%	27.3%	22.9%
Disagreed with statement (1, 2, or 3 on scale)	66.7%	47.3%	56.9%
Neutral (4 on scale)	14.8%	25.5%	20.2%

edge; and minimizing changes in staff, policies, and procedures has a dramatic, positive effect on postevent performance.

These tables separate the respondents into two groups: those reporting one or more postevent problems and those reporting no such problems. The accompanying Figures 8 through 11 are more specific, correlating responses to the statements above with *particular* postevent problems.

Figure 8 evaluates *worker productivity*. It shows a far greater incidence of productivity losses among companies that failed to keep employees informed of premerger developments, that kept human resources managers out of premerger planning, and that changed staff, policies, and procedures in a manner that impacted negatively on employee morale.

Figure 9 evaluates *market share*. It shows that keeping employees informed has little effect on

34

the newly formed organization's market share, but a higher incidence of lost market share among companies that excluded the human resources function from premerger planning, or lowered employee morale through changes in staff, policies, and procedures.

Figure 10 evaluates *profitability*. It shows, again, that keeping employees informed has a lesser effect on profitability than do the other two factors.

Figure 11 evaluates *employee turnover*. It shows that employee turnover was a far greater problem to firms that did not keep their people informed of premerger developments, that excluded human resources managers from the planning process, or that changed staff, policies, and procedures to the dissatisfaction of their employees.

One Thing Leads to Another

The effect of poor communication, internal changes, and management turnover is cumulative. Each creates employee dissatisfaction; that dissatisfaction, in turn, creates measurable problems that show up on the bottom line.

Faulty policies do not have an equal impact on the newly formed organization. Looking for specifics, the AMA questionnaire presented this statement, and asked for responses on a 7–to–1 scale:

> The following factors contributed strongly to employee dissatisfaction:
>
> 1. Lack of timely communication from senior management
> 2. Discrepancies in salary and benefits programs
> 3. Workforce reductions
> 4. Changes in staff, policies, and procedures
> 5. Management turnover

Table 13 gives the figures for all respondents.

The cumulative effect on the newly formed organization can be seen in Figure 12, which compares average responses among 32 firms reporting multiple postevent problems with those from 77 firms reporting only one such problem, or none at all. The conclusion: poor communication from senior management is the leading cause of problems when companies tie the corporate knot.

Table 12. "Changes in staff and in policies and procedures had a serious negative impact on employee morale."

	Companies reporting postevent problems	Companies reporting no such problems	All
Average on 7-point scale	4.20	2.76	3.49
Mode on 7-point scale	3	1	1, 2, & 3
Agreed with statement (5, 6 or 7 on scale)	42.6%	20.0%	31.2%
Disagreed with statement (1, 2, or 3 on scale)	40.7%	72.7%	56.9%
Neutral (4 on scale)	16.7%	7.3%	11.9%

Figure 8. Respondents evaluating postevent losses in worker productivity

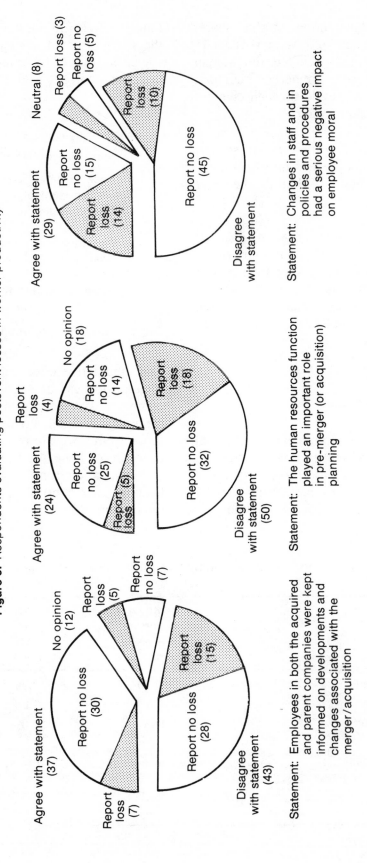

Statement: Employees in both the acquired and parent companies were kept informed on developments and changes associated with the merger/acquisition

Statement: The human resources function played an important role in pre-merger (or acquisition) planning

Statement: Changes in staff and in policies and procedures had a serious negative impact on employee moral

Figure 9. Respondents evaluating postevent losses in market share

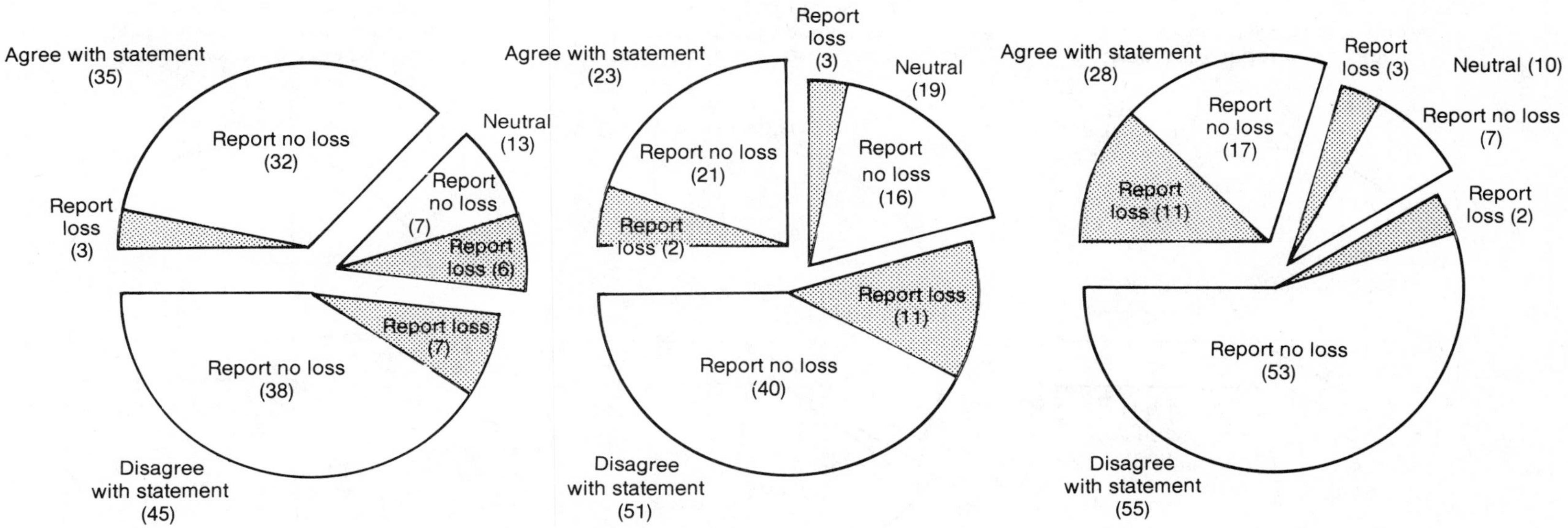

Statement: Employees in both the acquired and parent companies were kept informed on developments and changes associated with the merger/acquisition

Agree with statement (35)
Report no loss (32)
Report loss (3)
Neutral (13)
Report no loss (7)
Report loss (6)
Report loss (7)
Report no loss (38)
Disagree with statement (45)

Statement: The human resources function played an important role in pre-merger (or acquisition) planning

Agree with statement (23)
Report no loss (21)
Report loss (2)
Neutral (19)
Report loss (3)
Report no loss (16)
Report loss (11)
Report no loss (40)
Disagree with statement (51)

Statement: Changes in staff and in policies and procedures had a serious negative impact on employee moral

Agree with statement (28)
Report no loss (17)
Report loss (11)
Report loss (3)
Neutral (10)
Report no loss (7)
Report loss (2)
Report no loss (53)
Disagree with statement (55)

Figure 10. Respondents evaluating postevent losses in profitability.

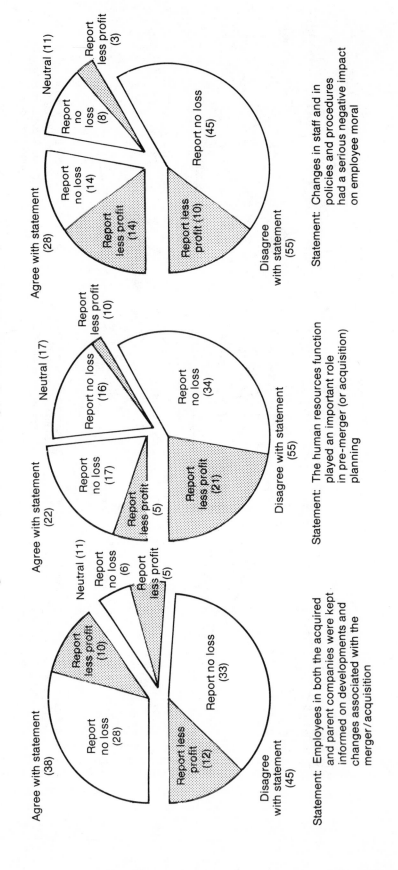

Statement: Employees in both the acquired and parent companies were kept informed on developments and changes associated with the merger/acquisition

Statement: The human resources function played an important role in pre-merger (or acquisition) planning

Statement: Changes in staff and in policies and procedures had a serious negative impact on employee moral

Figure 11. Respondents evaluating postevent worker turnover.

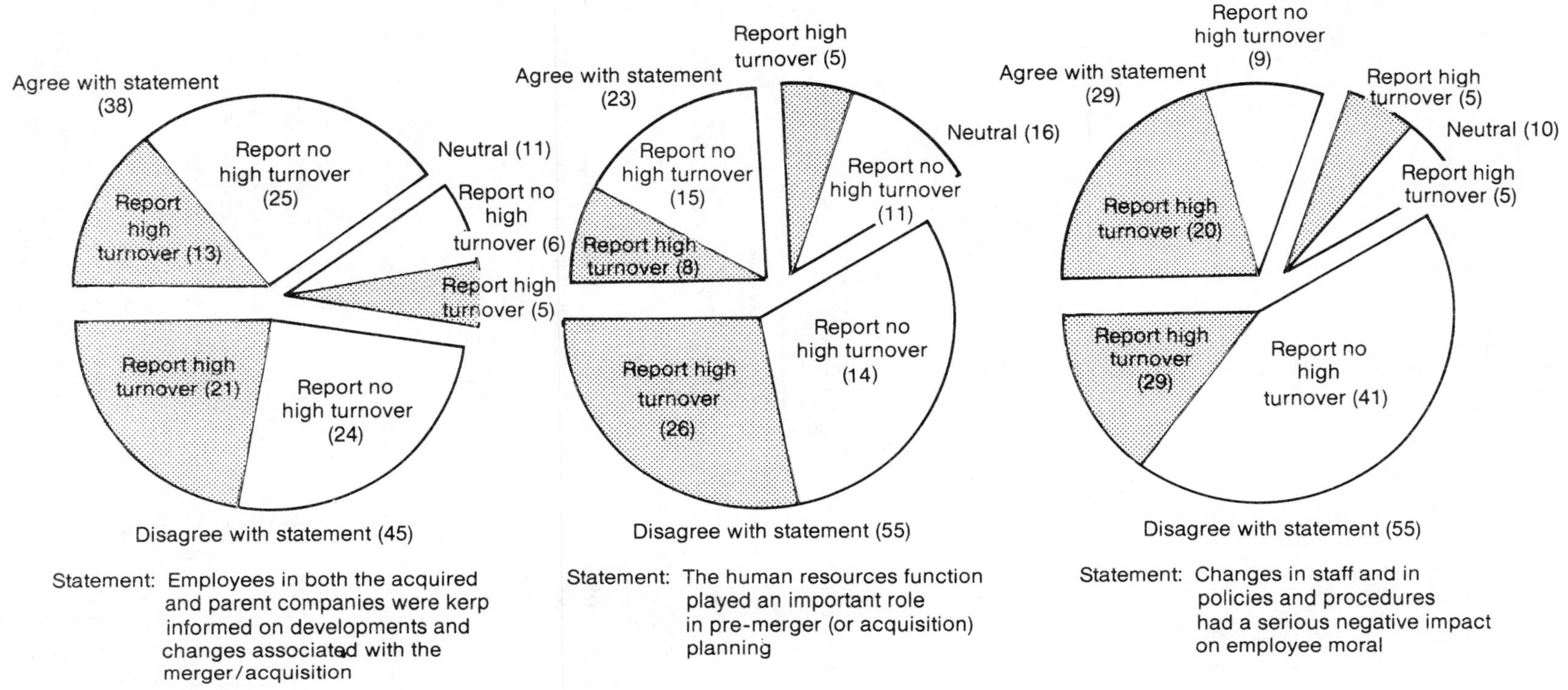

Agree with statement
(38)

Report no
high turnover (25)

Report high
turnover (13)

Report no
high turnover (24)

Report high
turnover (21)

Neutral (11)

Report no
high
turnover (6)

Report high
turnover (5)

Disagree with statement (45)

Statement: Employees in both the acquired
and parent companies were kerp
informed on developments and
changes associated with the
merger/acquisition

Agree with statement
(23)

Report no
high turnover
(15)

Report high
turnover (8)

Report high
turnover (5)

Report no
high turnover
(11)

Report no
high turnover
(14)

Report high
turnover
(26)

Neutral (16)

Disagree with statement (55)

Statement: The human resources function
played an important role
in pre-merger (or acquisition)
planning

Report high
turnover (5)

Neutral (10)

Report high
turnover (5)

Report no
high turnover
(9)

Agree with statement (29)

Report high
turnover (20)

Report no
high
turnover (41)

Report high
turnover
(29)

Disagree with statement (55)

Statement: Changes in staff and in
policies and procedures
had a serious negative impact
on employee moral

Table 13. Factors contributing to employee dissatisfaction.

	Average	Agree	Disagree	Neutral
Lack of timely communication	3.73	40.2%	48.5%	11.2%
Management turnover	3.58	38.3	45.8	15.9
Changes in staff, policies, and systems	3.74	36.4	43.0	20.6
Workforce reductions	3.46	28.9	49.6	21.5
Discrepancies in salary and benefits	3.07	22.4	56.9	21.5

Figure 12. What conditions contributed to employee dissatisfaction?

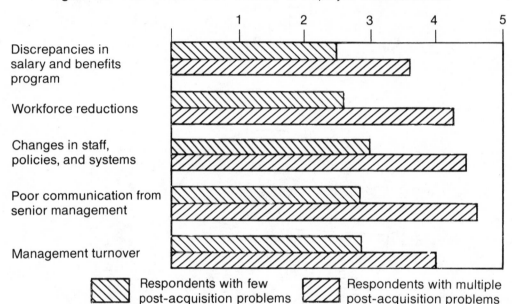

Notes: Respondents agreed/disagreed with statements related to each category, using a seven-point scale. The figure uses averages on that scale to chart impact on morale.

IMPACT: THE INFORMATION SYSTEMS FUNCTION

Senior managers often display a sublime faith in the ability of their computer professionals to overcome technological problems in management information systems. Where computers are concerned, miracles seem routine. Lacking an intricate understanding of the technology, CEOs often downplay the difficulties of merging systems. Somehow, they are sure, the wizards in MIS will work things out.

This attitude is underlined by a finding reported above, and depicted in Figure 2: fewer than half the respondents in the AMA sample had full information on the target company's computer hardware systems, and fewer than a third had full information on computer software systems or voice and data communications systems in advance of the merger or acquisition. Compared with financial data, with production and sales figures, and even with human resources matters (salary scales, benefits packages, and stock option plans), information systems are a low priority to parent or acquiring firms.

But systems incompatibility correlates highly with postevent problems. Companies dealing with incompatibilities in various information systems, especially in such functions as general administration, human resources, purchasing, and production and distribution, reported a far higher incidence of the problems listed in the questionnaire than did firms reporting no such incompatibilities. The correlation was especially high among manufacturing companies that faced incompatibilities in production systems. Moreover, respondents that set a high priority on merging incompatible systems found themselves with fewer postevent problems.

This section of the AMA questionnaire began by asking:

> After the merger/acquisition, in which functions did system incompatibility prove a problem?

Depending on the function, incompatibility proved a problem for anywhere from 19 to 31 percent of respondents. At the high end were general ledger systems (31.2 percent) and general and administrative systems; at the low end, human resources systems (22 percent) and purchasing (19.3 percent).

But where incompatibilities did occur, so also did reports of postevent problems. To underline the figures displayed in Table 14: companies that faced incompatibilities in general and administrative systems were four times more likely to report postevent problems than were others; in purchasing systems, three times more likely; in human resources systems, two and one-half times more likely. And among manufacturing firms, those with incompatibilities in production and distribution systems were *12 times* more likely to report postevent problems.

Setting Priorities

Not all respondents felt it necessary to merge every one, or even any, of their systems. But the drive to centralize forced many newly wedded companies to set priorities. The AMA questionnaire listed six sets of functional systems and asked respondents:

Table 14. Postevent incompatibilities in information systems.

System Incompatibilities	Pct. of companies reporting postevent problems	Pct. of companies reporting no such problems	Pct. of all
General ledger	37.0	25.5	31.2
General administrative	48.2	12.7	30.3
Accounts payable/receivable	31.5	23.7	27.5
Benefits	31.5	21.8	26.7
Payroll	29.6	20.0	24.8
Human resources	31.5	12.7	22.0
Purchasing	29.6	9.1	19.3
Production/distribution (manufacturing firms only)	41.2	3.6	7.3

What priorities did you establish in merging systems? Please identify the highest priority with a 1, and continue with 2, 3, 4, 5 and 6 in order of decreasing importance.

Table 15 displays the results.

Two factors were at work where companies set priorities. The first and most obvious involved a judgment call based on the perceived *importance* of merging various functional systems. As is obvious in Table 15, the financial and operational functions rated highest.

The other factor: incompatibility. Respondents dealing with incompatible systems were quick to set priorities; others were not. Cases in point:

- Of 40 firms that faced incompatibilities in financial systems, 37, or 92.5 percent, established priorities. Of 69 firms that reported no compatibility problems in financial systems, only 43, or 62.3 percent, established priorities.
- Of 42 firms facing incompatibilities in operational systems, 41 established a priority system; of 67 reporting no compatibility problems, only 38 established priorities.
- *All* 24 firms that faced incompatibilities in human resources systems established a priority system; of 85 reporting no

compatibility problems, only 48 established a priority system.

A Matter of Time

Though incompatibility made respondents quick to set priorities in merging systems, it naturally slowed down their ability to merge them. As Figure 13 reveals, nearly 80 percent of the 34 companies that reported no incompatibility problems had their systems in sync within six months of the merger or acquisition. Conversely, a third of the 65 companies reporting incompatibilities in one or more systems took more than a year to resolve the problem.

There is a very high correlation between the amount of time spent merging systems and the report of postevent problems. Table 16 displays the figures.

The key reading in Table 16: loss of market share. Of the 16 respondents who lost market share in the wake of the merger or acquisition, 13 took more than six months to merge systems. The finding is even more dramatic in the manufacturing sector. Of the 19 manufacturers who merged their systems within six months of the event, only one reported a loss of market share; of the 20 manufacturers who took more than six months to merge systems, 6 reported a loss of market share.

In view of the vital necessity of merging sys-

Table 15. Establishing priorities in merging systems.

Systems	1st	2nd	3rd	4th	5th	6th	Not reported
Financial	44	19	10	5	0	2	29
Operational	18	34	10	7	8	2	30
Human resources	3	8	21	15	27	1	34
Payroll	11	8	19	23	11	2	35
Benefits	2	7	13	24	27	2	34
Other	1	1	1	0	1	62	43

Figure 13. Time spent merging systems (in months).

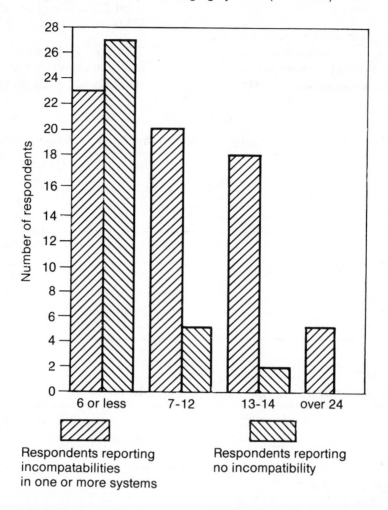

Respondents reporting
incompatabilities
in one or more systems

Respondents reporting
no incompatibility

tems quickly, companies may opt for outside help. The questionnaire asked:

> Was a service bureau used to handle some data processing due to limited or strained MIS capacity?

Sixteen respondents, or 14.7 percent of the sample, said yes. An additional 19 (17.4 percent) considered using a service bureau but decided against it. Most (67.9 percent) neither employed nor considered using a service bureau.

But firms might decide differently a second time around, according to Table 17.

Paying the Bill

Most respondents encountered no expenditures on information systems that were directly attributable to the merger or acquisition. Where necessary, however, the ticket tended toward the high side. Nine firms had major expenditures, amounting to $50,000 or more in hardware costs and a like amount in software costs.

The questionnaire asked:

> What MIS expenditures were directly attributable to the merger/acquisition?

The responses, detailed in Table 18 below, are here summarized:

Hardware. 14.7 percent of respondents made computer hardware expenditures attributable to the merger/acquisition. One respondent spent as little as $5,000; another, as much as $500,000. About half spent $50,000 or less; about half spent $75,000 or more on hardware.

Software. 17.4 percent of respondents made computer software expenditures attributable to the merger/acquisition.

Table 16. Correlation of time spent merging systems to incidence of postevent problems.

Postevent problems	Time Spent in Merging Systems (in months)			
	1–6 (50)	7–12 (25)	13–24 (20)	+24 (5)
No such problem reported	64%	36%	20%	40%
One or more problems reported	36	64	80	60
Loss in worker productivity	20	24	40	60
Loss in market share	6	28	20	40
Lesser profitability	36	40	30	40
High employee turnover	24	48	60	40

Table 17. Decision to employ a service bureau, past against future.

In past:	In future mergers/acquisitions:	
	Would consider employing an SB	Would not consider employing an SB
Employed a service bureau	68.8%	31.3%
Service bureau considered, but not employed	72.7	27.3
Service bureau neither considered nor employed	35.0	65.0

Pcts. are of companies in each *past* category who responded to query about future use of service bureaus.

Table 18. MIS expenditures directly attributable to merger/acquisition.

	Hardware	Software	Training
None reported	93	90	94
$1,000 to $5,000	1	2	5
$6,000 to $10,000	2	1	2
$11,000 to $25,000	2	6	3
$26,000 to $50,000	3	5	2
$51,000 to $75,000	2	1	0
$76,000 to $100,000	1	3	1
$101,000 to $250,000	4	0	1
$251,000 to $500,000	1	1	1

One respondent spent as little as $1,200; another, as much as $500,000. Half spent $25,000 or less; half spent $40,000 or more on software.

Training of non-MIS personnel. 13.8 percent of respondents had training expenditures directly attributable to the merger/acquisition. One spent as little as $3,000; another, as much as $300,000. Half spent $10,000 or less; half spent $25,000 or more on training.

SYSTEMS SOLUTIONS TO HUMAN RESOURCES ISSUES

Of all the areas in which premerger information is gathered, systems is clearly the least studied—and the least understood. Yet, not only is the acquired company's database an invaluable asset in solving many postmerger problems, it is the lifeblood of business information.

As noted previously in this report, whereas respondents had adequate premerger data regarding human resources issues, they frequently noted ignorance of systems functions, capabilities, and capacities. This deficiency resulted in lack of information on many aspects of the employee population and employee policies and practices, both of which impacted on good management of the transition. Systems, where managed properly, can provide such information resources. Compounding the transition problem for respondents was a tendency to avoid regular communications until all decisions were made and ready for implementation.

Many of the problems that impacted organizational life during and after the merger could often have been addressed by means of data systems in place. Degree of attention to the systems area varied among acquiring or merging companies. Said one respondent, "We historically have had problems in systems, so we made that a top priority. The consequences

were a smoother transition." Said another, "Had we anticipated the problems we ran into, things would have been handled more efficiently."

When respondents ranked areas to be merged, human resources, payroll, and benefits were rated three, four, and five in order of importance. Obviously, no company will have the time, systems, and staff capacity to handle adequately details in every area simultaneously. Fortunately, these three areas can be assisted by outside services. For example, whereas only 14.7 percent of respondents looked to outside information-processing firms for help during the transition, 36.7 percent said they would consider such help in the future. This indicates an awareness that using outside services in some areas such as payroll processing and tax filing can free operations staff for other priorities.

In addition, regardless of how businesses merge payroll systems, developing new and equitable pay systems can provide an opportunity to unify companies—especially when employees are involved in the process. The new compensation system can also provide a foundation for human resources information management in the new organization. The merger/acquisition can provide opportunity for addressing inefficiencies and other ills.

One merging retail organization received such a "fringe" benefit from the process. A company involved in a buyout situation had had a microbase service (which it allowed to lay dormant) and an HRIS mainframe service. In the process of being bought, its offices were moved from Minneapolis to Denver and the acquiring company implemented a LAN tie in. The newly formed company merged systems and at the same time implemented its own HRIS in six months. As a result, the more remote offices felt closer to headquarters and other subdivisions, and the company saw an additional "perk" in its new system. The old system had been inefficient at calculating many aspects of the employee benefits package. By integrating systems and then implementing the HRIS, the company was able to decide which benefits would be best, given its employee population, and was able to offer a new, much more attractive health care package.

Sometimes problems may seem virtually insurmountable, and there is little to be done about it but to forge ahead. "We had nightmares in the payroll systems," reported one respondent. "Our software was incompatible with theirs. There wasn't anything we could have done differently. It was just a matter of incompatibility."

Companies Who Love People

When asked about problems in merging systems, an overwhelming majority of respondents inevitably wound up talking about the "people aspects" of the merger. Said one, regarding the merging of systems, "Human resources are very important. You must pay attention to this area or else there won't be a smooth transition. We made sure that the employees were well informed about the new system. In addition, we tried to alleviate anticipation and rumors." Said another, "Merging systems and keeping people informed were top priorities for us because the employees are the lifeblood of our organization. Without them we are nothing, and all the rest is meaningless."

Communication and support were the dominant themes—not only at the lower levels but for managers as well. This may mean generating different kinds of reports and coaching managers on how to read them, who to forward them to, and so on. Commented one manager of an acquired company, "I literally felt I needed someone there to hold my hand just to get through all the reports. I had so many questions with no one to ask about them."

Asking the Right Questions of Your Database

There are a number of areas where businesses can use available systems resources in the human resources area to promote a smoother transition. They can:

- Analyze their employee populations in such areas as job classification, education, job performance, training, and experience to aid in strategic organizational planning and to identify redundancies. (In many companies, skills tend not to be captured in corporate systems.)
- Review labor costs using diverse scenarios to determine the need for a workforce realignment. Productivity measures can help determine which divisions generate the most revenue and which employees are most productive within each department. On this basis, the company can deploy employees to various divisions or departments and make decisions as to staff cuts if there are redundancies.

Job cost analyses will reflect what it costs to produce a job. By factoring in all elements, such as estimated labor hours, estimated labor cost, and estimated burden (overhead) cost (this can be predetermined, using a percentage of earnings, with each department having its own rate), and by tracking individuals assigned to every job, start and finish dates, and so on, individual productivity for each hourly worker can be derived. Make decisions based on thorough knowledge of both companies, and communicate the results to all employees.

Respondents could not emphasize strongly enough the importance of making this a careful process. Said one, "We lost a lot of good employees. We shouldn't have been so cold in our evaluation of [the acquired company's] employees. We should have been more encouraging." If performance problems with individuals are noted, it is often necessary, say respondents, to go beyond simply accepting these as criteria for making decisions. Is there a problem with a division manager? Is there some way we can help this employee to perform better? Getting to the root of the problem may mean talking to or counseling the employees in question, working on the individual level rather than relying merely on "paper" to make decisions.

■ Help employees understand that uniform criteria are being used in all decision-making processes. Employees should be assured that criteria are being applied without bias across the board and be informed as to what those criteria are. Management should reinforce the idea that decisions will not be arbitrary and that all available resources will be used.

When a corporation engages in several different types of businesses and operates in more than one state, the number of variables from a human resources and operations perspective can be compounded. Similarly, most diversified companies have more items to reconcile and maintain. Disparate pay rates, benefits programs, pension, profit-sharing and retirement programs, as well as union contracts and tax liabilities from state and local jurisdictions are among them.

Problems and Solutions

From the survey data and Control Data's experience in working with customers through mergers, acquisitions, and divestitures, one can identify five major problems in retrieving data and a number of solutions.

1. *Lack of information about what data are available; inability to determine the right questions to ask.*

Ask MIS managers or department heads for a full list and sample of available reports. Because they may also be able to create additional reports, it is important to understand what pieces of employee information are captured by internal and external systems. A listing of data elements will provide this.

2. *Incompatibility of systems and methods for organizing data.*

Allow systems to run separately unless the merger is meant to consolidate operations. In that case, notify employees of areas under consideration for change and set a timetable for implementation. The key word is communication. Also, outside consultants and service bureaus can help set up and maintain some records that can be merged or separated as needed.

3. *Low priority for operations and human resources issues.*

Include input from human resources, payroll, and MIS departments at the front end of the merger. CEOs need to ensure that these areas are not overlooked.

4. *Overload of information needs exceeding staff capacity.*

There are a number of ways to address an overload of programming and processing requests. After setting its information retrieval priorities, a company can hire additional programmers or MIS staff, retain temporary help, purchase new hardware and software adequate for the new company's needs, and/or look to outside help. For example, a 401(k) plan administered in-house could be done by a third-party administrator.

5. *Resistance from the acquired company's staff to retrieve information.*

This is perhaps the most difficult issue of all. Overall, there are no easy answers for the problems encountered during a merger, especially when it's a hostile takeover. But one thing is clear: openness and communication help pave the way for greater cooperation and future productivity. And information management is one of the best resources for setting the stage.

Note: The editors and project director wish to thank Bruce N. Croft, Gary Sewell, and Kathleen Davies of Control Data Business Management Services for their contributions to this section.

4

Gauging the Results

To most, but not all, of the companies polled, the success of a merger or acquisition is best gauged by the bottom line. The questionnaire listed *profitability*, *payback*, *market share*, and *other* (the last was open-ended), and asked:

> What are the best ways to determine the success of an acquisition or merger? Please identify the most important measure with a 1 and continue with 2, 3, and 4 in order of decreasing importance.

Table 19 displays the results.

It was no surprise to find that profitability ranked highest when companies measured the success of the merger or acquisition. In fact,

profitability proved an equally important measure of success among companies whose profits rose or remained constant after the event as it did among those reporting *lesser* profits. Among both groups, 40 percent rated "profitability" highest among success factors.

The same held true when we checked the figures on market share. We found no statistically significant difference in the ratings on "market share" as a success measure when we compared responses from companies that lost market share with those from the rest of the sample.

Where respondents wrote in some "other" criteria, bottom-line issues were often at play.

Table 19. Measuring success: respondent ratings.

Success factor	1st	2nd	3rd	4th
Profitability	39.8	40.7	11.1	6.5
Payback	36.1	26.9	22.2	13.0
Market share	10.2	24.1	54.6	9.3
Other	14.8	2.8	5.6	75.0

Six respondents rated "share price" and "shareholder value improvement" above profitability, payback, or market share as the most important measure of success. Three others ranked "cash flow" most highly (one was more specific: "cash flow to reduce debt"). Three more looked beyond the bottom line and gave top ranking to such write-in items as "accomplishes strategy," "reaching the specific objective," and "ongoing viability." And to one respondent, "job satisfaction" was paramount.

Other, less highly ranked criteria included "workforce security," "technology and products," "employee opportunity for advancement," and "employee attitudes one year later."

Time and Tide

Most AMA respondents feel that it takes more than one year, but less than five, for a merger or acquisition to prove itself successful. Figure 14 gives responses to the question:

> How long a time must pass before success can be properly measured?

Companies reporting postevent problems take a longer view on this matter than do the others. Only 26 percent of these firms say that success can be measured in two years or less, compared with 41 percent of the "no problem" group.

Time is money, and money matters greatly to the 109 companies in the AMA sample. As seen above, three out of four consider either profitability or payback the most important measure of success in the wake of a merger or acquisition. But if the eventual results are quantifiable, the processes that lead to the results are subject to a more qualitative analysis. The following section, built on follow-up telephone interviews with 70 respondents to the AMA questionnaire, provides such insights.

AVOIDING TOIL AND TROUBLE

The CEO and chief stockholder of a small East Coast consumer products company played his cards close to the chest. There was no need, he felt, to tell anyone that a takeover was imminent. Once the deal was consummated, he cleaned out his office, made his announcement, and walked out the door, leaving the company in chaos.

The new owner attempted to calm the waters. There would be no wholesale layoffs, the announcements said. Managers and others would be evaluated, individually, for their "worth" to the new company. "Unfortunately," noted the respondent, "employees found the announcements threatening. Good employees can always find work elsewhere, and that's exactly what they did—taking much needed information with them."

The new owner was able to put the company back together by contacting retirees and hiring them as consultants for the transition.

The story illustrates a flagrant disregard for what survey respondents see as the two most important keys for a successful acquisition: nurturing a productive relationship with top management in the company to be acquired, and managing communications as if the life of the venture depended on it. Other keys to success stem from these central themes. For example, respondents repeatedly underscored the importance of "understanding the company," anticipating problems, and having solutions ready to roll. Rapport with top management proved invaluable in this regard. After all, these are the individuals who understand the company best.

These conclusions emerged from approximately 70 interviews conducted with individuals who returned the questionnaire. Our researchers divided the respondents into two groups, based on the severity of problems (high

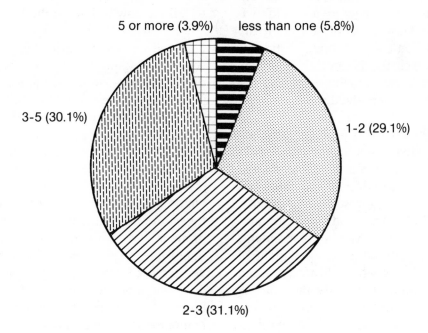

Figure 14. Time needed to measure success.
(in years)

5 or more (3.9%)   less than one (5.8%)

3-5 (30.1%)

1-2 (29.1%)

2-3 (31.1%)

turnover, loss of market share, etc.) encountered after the merger or acquisition. With those respondents who found themselves managing a troubled venture, we probed for insight into how the problems could have been avoided. Respondents in the second group were asked to talk about what actions they had taken to anticipate problems, and to share specifics on how they had managed a relatively trouble-free transition.

Our researchers analyzed the answers for major themes; the box on page 52 presents the results. Subtle but important differences, both in content and emphasis, are readily apparent. Respondents from the less-than-successful ventures repeatedly emphasized the importance of preacquisition homework and planning. Respondents in the second group, perhaps taking the homework stage for granted, showed a greater tendency to talk about the rapport they had built with management in the acquired company. Although both groups emphasized the role of communication, those who

had managed smoother transitions focused more intensely on the "people issues"—empathy with employees at all levels of the acquired company and ongoing meetings, both before and after the merger. The crucial factor, however, is that the vast majority of trouble-free transitions were "friendly" takeovers, an essential foundation for dialogue between managements, for understanding the company, and for providing a "win-win" framework.

Let's take a look at some of the major themes.

DON'T ASK FOR HEADACHES

The best way to avoid trouble, say respondents, is not to ask for it. Don't buy problems that can't be easily fixed. Evaluate the incompatibilities beforehand; be prepared to cancel the deal if these seem insurmountable. Avoid unionized companies. Don't buy into markets that you don't understand—this is clearly asking for trouble.

The more thorough the preacquisition homework, the fewer the problems. As one respondent put it, "You need to acquire a vast knowledge, an infinite knowledge of the company and the market you are entering." Said another, "We research the project exhaustively before we jump in; we know the company top to bottom before we make the deal."

Implicit in the homework is problem anticipation. One respondent uses an industrial psychologist to anticipate "worst case" scenarios, thus preparing itself to address and calm employees' fears regarding job security, benefits, and the like. "Without this advance preparation, we would flounder." Another respondent, prior to the merger, hired a vice president of human resources, reporting directly to the CEO, who did nothing but study the policies and benefits at the target company. Recommendations on how to deal with incompatibilities were drafted well in advance of the merger.

Among other problems to be anticipated, respondents cited:

Marketing. Either they did not understand the market they had acquired their way into, or management lacked "hands on" experience in that market. One CEO said frankly that he had misjudged the acquired company's position in the market.

Turnover. Some loss of the employee base may be inevitable. Having the machinery in place for replacing key positions quickly is critical.

Big Is Big; Small Is Small. And the two do not often meet on compatible ground, leading to clashes between the entrepreneurial spirit of an acquired company and the bureaucratic needs of the new parent. "You can't take top management from a big corporation and expect them to perform well in a smaller company, and have the entrepreneurial capabilities needed," noted one respondent. Or, as another respondent, the general manager of a recently

acquired small company put it, "I wish they would have given me a coach for a week, just to tell me how to handle the paper."

Nor will time necessarily heal the conflict between large and small. "We didn't anticipate problems because of our gradual approach of incorporating new ideas," said the spokesman for a parent corporation. "But even after a year, the employees had closed minds. They have a small company mentality and feel like our ideas are a bureaucratic encroachment."

On a more positive note, one might say that it takes an entrepreneur to understand an entrepreneur. "We only acquire small companies," noted one respondent. "The largest company we acquired had only 400 employees. All of our key management spent time getting to know everyone before the merger. I think our company runs under an ideal system (entrepreneurial) and that companies are very happy when they merge into our system."

One respondent noted, however, that "small" does always equate with "entrepreneurial." His company had recently acquired a small division previously owned by a *Fortune* 500 company. He expected to run the new acquisition on a "hands off" basis, only to find it floundering for lack of direction. The previous parent had left its mark on company culture—tight control was an expectation.

Problems with Clients and Customers. "I realize now that we should have given more attention to our clients and the clientele of the company being acquired," said one respondent in the financial services industry, with regret. "We should have kept in closer touch with our audience, keeping them briefed on what we planned to do in the merger."

Plant or Facility Consolidation. Many of the problems involved here cannot be anticipated, say respondents. Only one respondent tendered advice: "Work as quickly as possible to get in contact with the employees to discuss placement elsewhere in the company, retirement benefits, outplacement services, and the like. Be aware that the remaining employees are naturally insecure—where will the ax fall next?''

THE MANAGEMENT-TO-MANAGEMENT LINK

As noted previously, this subject emerged repeatedly in conversations with those who had managed relatively trouble-free ventures. These statements are representative:

> We did not incur any problems because when I took over the company, the contract stipulated that top management would remain for three years. I wanted them to stay on so that they could teach me. I was just an addition to the staff— and there was only a small amount of apprehension among the employees.

> I think that both our company's management and their's had good visions as to what needed to be accomplished. As a result, we were able to to combine these visions for a successful merger.

> Success is a matter of providing support to management—the management that is in place— in order to ensure improvements in the areas considered to be weaknesses. If management has contributed to identifying the weak spots, then it is much easier to provide support. By support, I mean moral and psychological support, not dumping in lots of money.

> We only take over companies that want to be sold—and where management will receive us openly. The employees know that they work for a company that wants to be taken over. That's the kind of situation we like.

Those respondents managing turnarounds were, of course, far less respectful of existing managements. "We have to change management and policies,'' noted one respondent, the majority of whose acquisitions were turnarounds. "We pretty much expect to have problems with employee turnover. We could, however, communicate better—or in a softer way . . . We do it in kind of a blunt manner, and it scares off a lot people.'' Other respondents involved with turnarounds echoed similar ideas. One respondent, the director of human resources for a company specializing in turnarounds, told of being ordered to send wholesale pink slips on Christmas eve. In another case, she was asked to fire the CEO on his birthday. These tactics—not to be taken as representative—were taking their toll on her morale and morale at headquarters. Turnover at that location was becoming a serious problem.

Even when management stays in place, the rapport building must go further.

KNOW WHAT'S HAPPENING IN THE TRENCHES

''I know now that I should have gotten to know the employees better,'' noted a respondent who saw productivity plummet in a newly acquired company. "I did get to know upper management well, but not the people who make the operation run.'' Others cited similar ideas:

> We believe that people who are right there in the trenches are the ones best equipped to make decisions about their areas—rather than someone who is five levels up. The people who do the work are the ones whom the company should look to for answers to problems.

> You should try to realize that employees are not themselves when their company is being taken over. They have tremendous stress and insecurity about their jobs, and you should be aware of this. I usually go out of my way to get to know

some of the lower level employees. I let them know what is going on, and they know me on a first-name basis. I think this helps a lot.

Respondents frequently linked "getting to know the company" with sensitivity to people. "How people are handled determines all aspects of the merger," noted one. "You must make people a high priority," said another. "They are the the business." Respondents with troubled mergers echoed the same idea, wisdom gained from hindsight:

> We had a rude awakening to the old idea that business is people, and people have to be motivated . . . We should have gotten more input from the company, and more attention should have been paid to the people.

> To put it bluntly, our company is not too concerned about people. The [merger] was purely a financial decision. After the merger, morale at the acquired company deteriorated.

Respondents underscored the importance of sensitivity to people during personnel evaluations. The elimination of redundant positions may be inevitable—and how the evaluations are announced and managed is of critical importance. Here, if anywhere, interpersonal skills are put to the acid test. Be "encouraging and supportive" was the advice most frequently proffered.

In evaluating management positions, one respondent reported success in using an outside appraisal service. "External management assessment is always better than internal," states this respondent, advising other firms to consider the same tactic.

COMMUNICATE, COMMUNICATE, COMMUNICATE

Asked to cite one key to a smooth transition, respondents who had managed such transitions mentioned communication twice as frequently as any other factor. Although written communication is important, meetings and one-on-one sessions are essential—and vastly more effective. One or two meetings won't accomplish the agenda; the sessions must be ongoing. Task forces and "employee-relations teams" play important roles. Advance planning is critical. Said one respondent, "We make the communication plan integral with the overall acquisition plan. We lavish as much (perhaps more) attention on this than on any other aspect of the plan." Other representative answers:

> Once the deal has been made, sit down with them and explain what is going to happen . . . and why. Keep them up to date, and a little later, sit down with them, one on one, so they can express their opinions and ask questions.

> We met with the personnel staff at each location and actually made them into an executive group. We met repeatedly with each group, then had a meeting with all the groups together.

> We gave the employees booklets telling them about our company and our philosophy. We gave them a question-and-answer sheet and also a video tape about our company. We held a formal reception with our president and CEO and their employees so that they felt we cared about them.

Opinions differed on the worth of staging meetings prior to the merger. Stated one respondent who made such meetings part of his plan, "When we would ask if anyone had questions, there weren't any. We found out that they had to work with the information for a while before they had questions—and then we were flooded."

Respondents representing acquired companies echoed the same needs. "Their management did an excellent job of explaining the benefits and policies to us. They took each of us to dinner for an initial meeting with the corporate

HR person, then sat with us as a group for questions and answers. My only advice—they should have continued the exercise further down the ladder, all the way to the shop floor. They assumed that if the managers understood the benefits, it would filter down. Not true.''

Respondents from acquired companies emphasized the importance of dispatching a ''coach'' from the parent corporation. ''The only difference, now that we're 'owned,' is that we have more reports and more overhead. During those first months, I needed someone to walk me through the procedures—who gets what report, for example.'' Said another, ''They should have dispatched a team and had them live with us for a while. It would have helped tremendously.''

Respondents repeatedly called attention to both the tone and the content of the communication meetings, ''supportive'' and ''optimistic'' being the key themes. ''We had some very exciting growth plans for the acquired company, and we wanted the employees to share that excitement,'' as one respondent put it.

KEEP A LIGHT HAND ON THE CONTROLS

In view of the foregoing, it comes as no surprise that respondents with a lower incidence of problems managed the new acquisition with a light hand. Given their tendency to look for compatibility, to avoid problem companies, and to emphasize rapport with the acquisition's management, a ''hands off'' management style worked well. The idea that ''if it's not broken, don't fix it'' recurred repeatedly. Many respondents, however, indicated that controls might well be tightened in the future. Representative answers:

> When we acquire a company that is a well run, good company, we don't try to implement any changes for a long while . . . letting everyone get used to us first. Of course, if a company isn't running well and needs changes immediately, we do that, too.

> We don't move in right away and dictate what's going to happen. We let them run their operations as they have been. We may tighten things slowly as we go along. After a while, we may put one or two people into the company, to ensure that we have a reliable source of information.

Summary of Interview Findings

Answers given in order of descending frequency
Question: Looking back, how might the problems have been anticipated?

- *Better homework.* Know the market, know the workers, know the business needs.
- *Better planning.* Set a game plan from day one, but give sufficient lead time for implementation; know what problems to expect, and work to solve them; consolidate administrative areas quickly.
- *Better communication.* Be sensitive to employee needs; provide clear statements of direction; emphasize cooperation; be optimistic and supportive. Above all, make the communication ongoing.

Base: 32 respondents currently managing problem mergers or acquisitions.

Question: To what extent did you anticipate problems, especially in the employee-relations area? Specifically, what did you do that helped the transition?

- *Manage communication.* Maintain constant involvement; keep it ongoing, with all channels open. Use meetings whenever possible; pay attention to employee fears.
- *As much as possible, leave things the same.* Act as a consultant; if it's not broken, don't fix it.
- *Keep management in place for a specified time.* Provide incentives to stay; build moral and psychological support.
- *Avoid problem companies.* Buy into compatible and relatively problem-free companies.
- *Homework.* Extensive and exhaustive. Use external consultants, as appropriate.

Base: 38 respondents reporting relatively trouble-free mergers.

Appendix

**COMPREHENSIVE CHECKLIST FOR AN
ACQUISITION**

I. *Corporate Background*
 1. Original name and purpose
 2. Date of founding
 3. Subsequent changes in corporate name or purpose
 4. Brief description of present business
 5. Classes of stocks or other securities
 6. Concentration of ownership
 7. Activity of shares and price ranges (if traded)
 8. Subsidiaries and operating investments
 9. States in which qualified to do business
 10. Location of all facilities
 11. Board minutes review

II. *Basis of Proposed Acquisition*
 1. Highlights of agreement
 2. Formula for evaluation of shares
 3. Determination of real motive for willingness to merge or be bought

III. *Financial*
 1. General
  A. Source and authenticity of financial data
 2. Financial status
  A. Detailed consolidated financial statements
   1. Past 5 years and current year-to-date actual results (including monthly results and results vs. plan for last 12 months)
   2. Past 5 years and current year-to-date actual results by business segment
  B. Strategic plans, if any
   1. Current 5 year strategic plan including

    a. Financial projections, both consolidated and consolidating

    b. Underlying assumptions

   2. Past strategic plans, if any

  C. Current and past fiscal year budgets (include breakout and allocation of corporate and divisional overhead expense)

  D. Analysis of assets

   1. Cash position—monthly for past 2 years

   2. Projection of cash activity over next 6 months

   3. Accounts receivables aging schedule. Also condition, turnover, bad debts, experience and reserve. Analyze previous years

   4. Investments (kinds, condition, and basis for evaluation)

   5. Officers and employees loans (amounts and situations)

   6. Analysis of prepaid expenses

   7. Analysis of deferred charges

   8. Listing of manufacturing facilities, including equipment and real estate owned and leased

   9. Goodwill (basis of valuation)—amortization period

  E. Analysis of liabilities

   1. Schedule of current and projected indebtedness, including mandatory debt retirement

   2. Bank loans—for previous 5 years

   3. Accounts payable (include policy of discounts)

   4. Special reserves

   5. Contingent liabilities:

    a. Existing and threatened law suits

    b. Existing or potential environmental litigation

    c. Notes and obligations guaranteed

    d. Liability under major purchase contracts

    e. Other commitments

   6. Bank lines of credit available—terms, rates, etc.

   7. Status of income taxes (federal, state, and local)

   8. Trend and status of real estate and personal property taxes

  F. Information regarding preferred stock

  G. Information regarding major suppliers, by location and product type, including historical and projected dollar volume of products supplied

3. Financial operations

  A. Income statement for past 5 years

  B. Analysis of sales and income

   1. Sales by product by year over last 5 years

   2. Sales by product by month over last 2 years

   3. Present backlog by product

   4. Other income

  C. Analysis of expenses

   1. Selling expenses

   2. Administrative expenses

   3. General expenses

4. Possible economies in all expenses
5. Royalties received and paid
D. Analysis of income from domestic and international operations
   1. Profits by divisions, products, etc.
   2. Deductions
   3. Final operating net income
E. Analysis of net income
   1. Income from operations
   2. Details of income from other sources
   3. Deductions and taxes
   4. Final net income
F. Earnings record for 5-year period
   1. Cash gains or losses from operations
   2. Total gains or losses from operations
   3. Earnings in percent of sales
   4. Earnings in percent of invested capital
G. Dividend record for 5-year period
   1. Kind and amount of dividends paid
   2. Percent of earnings paid out in dividends by years
H. Energy problems—effect on operations
   1. Supply problems—list sources and contracts
   2. Cost problems
I. Historical and projected tax and book depreciation and amortization schedules through 1993
J. Breakdown by major category of capital expenditures and R&D expenditures over the past 5 years and projected for 5 years

IV. *Financial Controls*
   1. Kind of cost system employed
   2. Budget of sales, cost, profits, cash requirements, etc.
   3. Method of sales, administrative and general
   4. Method of controlling capital expenditures
   5. Historical projected working capital requirements
   6. Status of operating procedures—obtain any copies of accounting manuals, corporate procedures, etc.
   7. Adequacy of internal checks
   8. List of control reports issued
   9. Accounting methods employed
   10. Use of office machines, including data processing
   11. Financial rating (from reputable credit and banking facilities)
   12. Policies used in determining capitalization of fixed assets, deferred charges, reserves for write off of bad debts, amortization, and depreciation
   13. Information available on competitors, by geographic location

V. *Marketing Check List for Operational Analyses of Potential or New Acquisitions*
   (Note: The word "service" may be used interchangeably with the word "product")
   1. Product
   A. Description of products or product lines

B. Sales, cost of sales, gross profit, share of overall company sales, and gross profit for each product or product line

C. Sales by geographic trading area and share of market in each geographic trading area for each product or product line

D. Product superiority and weakness in relation to competitive products

E. Potential by-products or related products; obsolescence that may occur by competitive improving, or nature of customer demand

F. Compatability or conflict with present products and how new and present ones may be combined

2. Sales
   A. Distribution system
      1. If the company uses its own sales force (by product group or geographical area or centralized)—how organized (regional and branch offices); how many salespeople; territories; number of accounts; sales calls and orders; compensation (salary, commission, etc.); sales hiring and training policies and practices
      2. If noncompany "sales rep" organization—information as to rep organization, sales volume, other products handled, compensation
      3. If "wholesale" (not direct to consumer selling)—name, number, territory, compensation, and sales record of distributors; other products handled, if any
   B. Ability to mesh new products into existing channels of distribution, or present products into distribution system of new company

3. Markets
   A. Major competitors (name, location, size, industry status, strengths, and weaknesses)
   B. Major customers (name, location, volume in relation to total longevity, profit ability)
   C. Major suppliers of components, raw materials, etc. (name, location, longevity, dependability, quality, cost)
   D. Total potential market, growth or decline (factors affecting), and plans to attain larger shares
   E. Possible market areas of conflict or compatibility with present product markets
   F. Probable market stability or fluctuation; seasonality; "one shot" characteristics

4. Support services
   A. Advertising and sales promotion
      1. Agency or in-house department
      2. Organization and personnel (including compensation)
      3. Dollars budgeted and spent
      4. Sample ads, brochures, give-aways, trade shows, incentive or premium programs . . .
      5. How is public relations handled? Budget; results
   B. Market research
      1. In-house or outside services; organization and personnel, dollars budgeted and spent
      2. Copies of market-customer-product studies for evaluation as to growth potential, problem areas, follow-up action

5. Customer relations
   A. Customer longevity or turnover

APPENDIX

B. Customer comments, if any, as to reputation, quality, services, etc.
C. Planned activities to retain goodwill, e.g. customer service training

VI. *Management and Industrial Relations*
(Refer to Separate Checklist)

VII. *Facilities*
1. Real properties
   A. Locations
   B. Descriptions
   C. Title abstracts
   D. Title opinions
   E. Title insurance
   F. Surveys
   G. Encumbrances, liens, or charges (including tax liens, mortgages, rights of way and easements, restrictions, reversions zoning laws, and local ordinances)
2. Real property leases
   A. Name of other party
   B. Location, description, and use
   C. Date, term, and termination rights
   D. Rent per month
   E. Guaranties
   F. Defaults or breaches
   G. Assignability
3. Personal property
   A. Lists of all equipments, trucks, cars, etc.
   B. Existence of any chattel mortgages, conditions sales contracts, or other liens
   C. Where government contracts are involved, are any assets the property of the U.S. government?
4. Intangibles/regulatory guidelines
   A. Patents, inventions, and know-how
      1. List of patents
      2. Patent search
      3. Appraisal of strength of patent position
      4. Review of patent license agreements
      5. Determination of approach to invention disclosures
      6. Employee patent, trade secret, and nondisclosure agreements
   B. Review of trademarks, trade names, and copyrights
   C. Review of adherence to existing OSHA and environmental guidelines and regulations

VIII. *Legal (Review and collect copies of all contracts, etc.)*
1. Review of corporate charters
2. Review of bylaws
3. Review of minutes books
   A. Stock validly issued, fully paid, and nonassessable
   B. Outstanding stock options. Copy of stock option incentive plan, if any

61

    C. Warrants or other rights to purchase stock
    D. Restrictions on transfers of shares
    E. Bonus plans
    F. Employment agreements
    G. Employee retirement payments
    H. Any major or long-term commitments
    I. Any other operating details of importance, such as the grant of exclusive licenses, franchises, state qualifications, etc.
4. Litigation summary and status report—review for insurance coverage
5. Review of functions of house counsel and outside counsel
6. Review for any legal problems peculiar to the company, product or service, or industry
7. Copies of all loans, agreements, bonds, and debentures
    A. Check restrictive covenants to determine conflict with acquirer's loan agreements bonds and debentures, and limitation on acquirer's conduct of business after acquisition
8. If broker involved, check
    A. Name and proof of authority to act
    B. Whose agent is the broker?
    C. Has written brokerage agreement specifying all terms been signed with broker?
    D. Who is to pay the commission—buyer or seller?
    E. Will there be an indemnification against brokerage claims?
9. Brochures and catalogs for all products
10. List of all environmental studies

IX. *Contracts (Obtain copies where feasible)*
  1. List by category
    A. License agreements
    B. Consulting contracts
    C. Union contracts
    D. Government contracts
    E. Distributorship agreements
    F. Contracts with customers
    G. Contracts with suppliers
    H. Employment contracts
  2. Review contracts for following:
    A. Assignability
    B. Possible antitrust violations
    C. Redetermination clauses
    D. Escalation
    E. Enforceability
    F. Breaches or defaults

X. *Insurance*
  1. Copies of all original policies. (Also include Worker's Compensation, disability, group benefits, and pensions)
  2. Three-year loss experience reports under all policies

3. If the policies are not immediately obtainable, a list of all such policies and information with respect to carriers, coverage, limits, policy term, annual premium, and brokers
4. Full information with respect to (a) any claims, whether existing or potential, and (b) law suits in excess of insurance limits
5. Memo regarding (a) any insurance changes either contemplated or in process, and (b) any insurance exposures
6. Names and locations of company officers and employees in charge of insurance programs
7. Names of brokers or consultants' business or personal relationships to any principals

XI. *Purchasing*
　　1. Purchasing policy manuals
　　2. Purchasing procedures
　　3. Who does purchasing? For whom?
　　4. Who is authorized to approve purchase requisitions and to what dollar limitation?
　　5. Types of materials, suppliers, and services purchased
　　6. List of current vendors
　　7. List of current vendors' price lists
　　8. Allowable trade discounts
　　9. Copies of purchase requisitions and purchase orders
　　10. Annual cost of purchases by category
　　11. Annual cost of purchasing department

XII. *Data Processing*
　　1. How much money is spent each year on the data processing function?
　　　A. List of all equipment owned outright, indicating
　　　　1. Year purchased
　　　　2. Amount/value
　　　B. List of all leased equipment, indicating
　　　　1. From which vendor
　　　　2. Amount/value
　　　　3. Length of commitment
　　　C. Additional equipment on order (purchase/lease)
　　　　1. From which vendor
　　　　2. Amount/value
　　　　3. Length of commitment
　　　D. List of all other mechanical equipment not in data processing area (exclude adding machines and normal calculators)
　　　E. Determination of how much floor space is devoted to data processing equipment.
　　2. Detailed organization chart of data processing department
　　　A. Length of service
　　　B. Salary breakdown
　　　C. Status report
　　　　1. Housekeeping, security, etc.
　　　　2. Documentation and controls
　　　　3. Listing and scheduling of reports, etc.